1   9/00

Understanding
I Know Why the Caged Bird Sings

The Greenwood Press "Literature in Context" Series

Understanding *To Kill a Mockingbird:* A Student Casebook to Issues, Sources, and Historical Documents
Claudia Durst Johnson

Understanding *The Scarlet Letter:* A Student Casebook to Issues, Sources, and Historical Documents
Claudia Durst Johnson

Understanding *Adventures of Huckleberry Finn:* A Student Casebook to Issues, Sources, and Historical Documents
Claudia Durst Johnson

Understanding *Macbeth:* A Student Casebook to Issues, Sources, and Historical Documents
Faith Nostbakken

Understanding *Of Mice and Men, The Red Pony,* and *The Pearl:* A Student Casebook to Issues, Sources, and Historical Documents
Claudia Durst Johnson

Understanding Anne Frank's *The Diary of a Young Girl:* A Student Casebook to Issues, Sources, and Historical Documents
Hedda Rosner Kopf

Understanding *Pride and Prejudice:* A Student Casebook to Issues, Sources, and Historical Documents
Debra Teachman

Understanding *The Red Badge of Courage:* A Student Casebook to Issues, Sources, and Historical Documents
Claudia Durst Johnson

Understanding Richard Wright's *Black Boy:* A Student Casebook to Issues, Sources, and Historical Documents
Robert Felgar

UNDERSTANDING
I Know Why the Caged Bird Sings

A STUDENT CASEBOOK TO ISSUES, SOURCES, AND HISTORICAL DOCUMENTS

Joanne Megna-Wallace

The Greenwood Press
"Literature in Context" Series
Claudia Durst Johnson, Series Editor

GREENWOOD PRESS
Westport, Connecticut • London

Library of Congress Cataloging-in-Publication Data

Megna-Wallace, Joanne, 1954–
    Understanding I know why the caged bird sings : a student casebook
to issues, sources, and historical documents / Joanne Megna-Wallace.
        p.   cm. — (The Greenwood Press "Literature in context"
series, ISSN 1074–598X)
    Includes bibliographical references and index.
    ISBN 0–313–30229–4 (alk. paper)
    1. Angelou, Maya. I know why the caged bird sings—Sources.
  2. Afro-American women authors—Biography—History and criticism—Sources.
    3. Women entertainers—Biography—History and criticism—Sources.
    4. Autobiography—Sources.   I. Title.   II. Series.
    PS3551.N464779   1998
    818'.5409
    [B]—DC21   97–48576

British Library Cataloguing in Publication Data is available.

Library of Congress Catalog Card Number: 97–48576
ISBN: 0–313–30229–4
ISSN: 1074–598X

First published in 1998

Greenwood Press, 88 Post Road West, Westport, CT 06881
An imprint of Greenwood Publishing Group, Inc.

Printed in the United States of America

The paper used in this book complies with the
Permanent Paper Standard issued by the National
Information Standards Organization (Z39.48–1984).

10 9 8 7 6 5 4 3 2 1

Contents

Introduction

The importance of Maya Angelou's autobiography *I Know Why the Caged Bird Sings* cannot be overestimated. Angelou's chronicle of an African American girl growing up in the rural South in the 1930s, written at the end of the turbulent decade of the 1960s, tapped into the conscience of a nation grappling with civil rights and women's liberation issues. In 1970 it was nominated for the National Book Award, and it soon became required reading at many high schools and colleges, a fact confirmed by the dubious distinction of its having been the frequent target of censorship. In 1995 the work topped the Office for Intellectual Freedom's "most challenged" list.

Following Angelou's appearance at President Bill Clinton's inauguration in 1993, where she read her poem "On the Pulse of Morning," interest in her work has intensified. In 1994, *I Know Why the Caged Bird Sings* was named among the one hundred best books for young adults by the Young Adult Library Services Association. As of August 1997, it had been on the *New York Times* paperback nonfiction bestseller list for 153 weeks. Also indicative of the book's popularity is the impact it has had on popular culture. The June 1995 issue of the *Alternative Law Journal* reported that a character in the film *Reality Bites* declares that he "knows why the caged bird sings" and that this line is also used "in a song on *Maxinquaye*, the new album by Tricky."

Angelou originally decided to write *I Know Why the Caged Bird Sings* because not enough had been written for young black girls in the United States. She wanted to remind her fellow African Americans that despite the obstacles and the pain they endured, there was much love and humor to be found in the African American community. Indeed, the book has a very definite appeal for young black girls. In a 1993 interview with Angelou, Oprah Winfrey described how important the work was to her because it was the first book she had read that reflected her own experience.

But despite her original intentions, Angelou found that when she began writing the book her ideas and audience changed: "I saw it was not just for black girls but for young Jewish boys and old Chinese women" (Julianelli, 124). The book's popularity endures not only because it continues to be instructive on matters of race and gender, but also because it is a universal tale of survival.

This study of *I Know Why the Caged Bird Sings* addresses both the specific and universal elements of Angelou's autobiography. It begins with a focus on the literary elements of *I Know Why the Caged Bird Sings*: its genre, central themes, point of view, setting, and so on. This literary analysis traces Angelou's journey from an awkward, lonely, and insecure child to an adolescent who survives many heartbreaks and emerges as a self-reliant and mature young woman. Subsequent chapters examine specific issues raised by the autobiography and the particular historical moment it portrays. Chapter 2 explores race relations in the post-Reconstruction, pre–civil rights South (the milieu of Angelou's childhood). Chapters 3 through 5 focus on institutions that have shaped African American culture in general and Angelou's experience in particular: the African American school under segregation, the African American church in the rural South, and the family. Chapter 6 considers the problem of sexual abuse (Angelou was raped at the age of seven), and Chapter 7 analyzes the issue of censorship. The bibliographic essay provides information on Angelou's activities, publications, and honors following the period portrayed in *I Know Why the Caged Bird Sings*.

A study such as this assumes that a work like *I Know Why the Caged Birds Sings* is not an isolated story of a single individual. It is rather a multilayered chronicle that can offer insight about the history and culture of a people at a particular time and place and that raises issues of profound and universal significance. The analyses contained in this study help to illuminate the historical context of the work and help us to understand more fully the issues it raises.

Chapters 2 through 7 include carefully selected documents that offer insight on a number of topics. Introductory material explains the relevance of each document or group of documents to *I Know Why the Caged Bird Sings*. Many of the documents published during the first half of the twentieth century shed light on the period in history about which Angelou writes. The documents have been drawn from many sources, including magazine and newspaper articles, interviews and first-person narratives, government publications, scholarly books and articles, legal statutes, and publications of nonprofit organizations. They reflect a wide variety of disciplines, among them literature, history, sociology, law, and music. Study questions, topics for written or oral exploration, and suggestions for further reading are also included.

Many people have contributed to bringing this project to fruition. I would like to thank, first of all, my husband, Chip Wallace, and my children, Patrick and Kelsey, for their patience, love, and support. I would also like to express my gratitude to Claudia D. Johnson, editor of the Literature in Context Series, and my colleague at Bradford College, Deborah Mistron, for their valuable comments and suggestions. Thanks also to the many librarians who have helped me: the library staff at Bradford College, especially Pat Paquette for her expertise and commitment to obtaining sources for me through interlibrary loan; and Sharon Snow, Curator of Rare Books at Wake Forest University, and Ellen Bard at the Central Arkansas Library System for their research efforts on my behalf. Finally, I would like to thank the many people who were instrumental in obtaining the necessary permissions to reprint material contained in this volume.

WORKS CONSULTED

Angelou, Maya. "Conversations with Oprah: Maya Angelou." *The Oprah Winfrey Show*, December 6, 1993. (Original airdate: July 13, 1993.) Transcript produced by *Burrelle's Information Services*.

Duff, Catherine, et al. "Maya Angelou." *Alternative Law Journal*, June 1995, 153.

Julianelli, Jane. "Maya Angelou." *Harper's Bazaar*, November 1972, 124.

Maryles, Daisy. "Strong Sellers in the NF Mass Market." *Publishers Weekly*, February 8, 1993, 14.

"Top One Hundred Countdown: Best of the Best Books for Young Adults." *Booklist*, October 15, 1994, 412–16.

Understanding
*I Know Why
the Caged Bird
Sings*

1

The Journey to Maturity and Self-Esteem: A Literary Analysis of Maya Angelou's *I Know Why the Caged Bird Sings*

THE AUTOBIOGRAPHICAL GENRE AND *I KNOW WHY THE CAGED BIRD SINGS*

In his analysis of Maya Angelou's autobiographical works, Selwyn R. Cudjoe asserts that African Americans have often chosen autobiography as their means of self-expression: "The Afro-American autobiographical statement is the most Afro-American of all Afro-American literary pursuits" (272). Cudjoe cites the autobiographies of Frederick Douglass, Linda Brent (Harriet Jacobs), Booker T. Washington, Zora Neale Hurston, Malcolm X, and W.E.B. Du Bois as testimony to "the strength, consistency, and importance of this genre in Afro-American literature" (277).

Slave narratives constitute the first written African American autobiographies. Slaves wrote in order to expose the horrific conditions under which they lived and to provide proof of their humanity to further the abolitionist cause. In her work *Where I'm Bound*, Sidonic Smith discusses the structural and thematic motifs established in the slave narratives, which she argues are repeated in subsequent African American autobiographies, including Angelou's. Smith writes: "The ex-slave narrated the story of his successful break *into* a community that allowed authentic self-expression and fulfillment in a social role. . . . He also narrated the story of his radical break *away from* an enslaving community that forbade him authentic selfhood" (ix).

In her anthology *Written by Herself*, Jill Ker Conway points to a dominant theme in black women's autobiography that is amply illustrated in *I Know Why the Caged Bird Sings*: "Because, from girlhood, these women faced the dual injustices of racial hostility and male exploitation, their life histories are told with no hint of romantic conventions. They describe, instead, a quest for physical and psychological survival" (3). Angelou's account of her childhood and adolescence chronicles her frequent encounters with racism, sexism, and classism at the same time that she describes the people, events, and personal qualities that helped her to survive the devastating effects of her environment. Despite the triple oppression she faced as a girl growing up poor in the racially segregated town of Stamps, Arkansas, Angelou stresses the role models and family members who sustained and nurtured her and the events that contributed to her development into a strong, independent young woman.

Angelou's rebellious spirit and zest for a challenge are revealed in an interview where she explained that she at first turned down the opportunity to write her autobiography, but was unable to resist when she was told that "to write an autobiography as literature is the most difficult thing anyone could do" (Tate, 6). When asked in the same interview how she selected the events presented in her autobiography, Angelou declared: "Some events stood out in my mind more than others. Some, though, were never recorded because they either were so bad or so painful, that there was no way to write about them honestly and artistically without making them melodramatic. They would have taken the book off its course" (Tate, 7).

Angelou's remarks suggest one of the complex issues involved in the analysis of autobiography. While autobiographers most likely intend to tell the truth about their own lives, they nevertheless make conscious decisions about what to include or exclude in order to write a coherent life. Conway notes, "Autobiographical narratives are fictions, in the same sense that the narrator imposes her or his order on the ebb and flow of experience and gives us a false sense of certainty and finality about causation in life." Despite this limitation, Conway goes on to assert the positive benefits of autobiographical narratives: "Yet they are not fictions but accounts of real lives, lived in a specific time and place, windows on the past, chances to enter and inhabit the real world of another person, chances to try on another identity and so broaden our own" (vii).

When asked whether she considers her autobiographical works to be novels or autobiographies, Angelou responds that they are autobiographies, suggesting that she has intended to write the truth about her life. But her response also alerts us to her intention to broaden her focus beyond her particular life to include a description of the historical moment she lived through: "When I wrote *I Know Why the Caged Bird Sings*, I wasn't thinking so much about my own life or identity. I was thinking about a particular time in which I lived and the influences of that time on a number of people. . . . I used the central figure—myself—as a focus to show how one person can make it through those times" (Tate, 6). Angelou's remarks are consistent with Cudjoe's analysis of the intentions of African American autobiography in general: "The autobiography . . . is meant to serve the group rather than glorify the individual's exploits. The concerns of the collective predominate and one's personal experiences are presumed to be the closest approximation of the group's experiences" (280).

For Angelou, the events she chooses to explore in her autobiography emphasize how she coped with her difficult life circumstances, and how others, too, can cope. She states: "All my work, my life, everything is about survival. All my work is meant to say, 'You may encounter many defeats, but you must not be defeated' " (Tate, 7). Angelou, then, writes from the perspective of a mature adult and crafts her work to convey the process of her development, to demonstrate how she overcame her personal defeats and survived.

This chapter considers several aspects of the work: we will explore the significant structural elements, including the episodic nature of the work, the importance of the time period and setting, and Angelou's use of language and tone. The second part of the analysis considers the specific events and the particular people whose love helped Maya to endure a childhood haunted by alienation and loneliness.

A STRUCTURAL AND DRAMATIC ANALYSIS OF
I KNOW WHY THE CAGED BIRD SINGS

Angelou's approach to her life story is roughly chronological, beginning with her arrival in Stamps at the age of three with her brother Bailey and concluding in California at the age of sixteen just after the birth of her son. Her story unfolds in a series of self-contained episodes that take place in various social settings. The opening scene is a carefully crafted description of an event that frames the entire work, defining the important thematic concerns that will be repeated throughout. The narrative opens with lines from a poem that attest to Maya's early sense of displacement: "What you looking at me for? I didn't come to stay . . ." (1). Her parents divorced when she was three years old, and their decision to send Maya and Bailey to live with their paternal grandmother contributes to Maya's low self-esteem and sense of not belonging. As many children do, Maya and Bailey feel that they are to blame for their parents' abandonment of them. Maya's sensitivity to the racism that permeates her environment further contributes to her sense of inferiority. Her sense of impotence and worthlessness is underscored in the opening pages when she dreams of waking up transformed into a beautiful white girl with blond hair and blue eyes. According to Smith, this "primal childhood scene brings into focus the nature of the imprisoning environment from which the self will seek escape. The black girl child is trapped within the cage of her own diminished self-image around which interlock the bars of natural and social forces" ("Song of a Caged Bird," 368).

This opening scene takes place in the Colored Methodist Episcopal Church, one of the predominant settings for Angelou's work. Angelou's narrative highlights the importance of the church as a social institution in her life and in the lives of the African Americans in her community, an issue that will be taken up in detail in Chapter 4 of this study. Other social institutions provide the setting for important episodes in the autobiography. Angelou's eighth-grade graduation furnishes a glimpse into the educational practices and environment of the Lafayette County Training School (see Chapter 3). The many interactions with the members of her immediate family provide important insights into the African American family as an institution (see Chapter 5). Scenes in her family's general store are occasions to explore all manner of social and economic interactions. It is in the store that Maya learns sympathy for the morning hopes and evening disappointments of the unfortunate cotton-pickers, where she witnesses her grandmother's painful encounter with the "powhitetrash" children, where she observes her grand-mother's resourceful bartering during the Great Depression, and where she gathers with her community to listen to Joe Louis's fight with Primo Carnera, a white boxer.

The periods of her life spent in St. Louis and San Francisco offer Angelou perspective on urban life. St. Louis introduces her to rel-atives who are streetwise, to strange new foods like thin-sliced ham, and to the hustle and bustle of city life. Living in San Fran-cisco adds to Angelou's knowledge of the ethics and behavior of the gamblers and con artists who frequent the black urban under-world.

The time period of the work is equally important. Angelou's de-scription of race relations in Stamps during the 1930s provides a vivid portrait of the "Jim Crow" era with its laws legalizing segre-gation and its unwritten rules governing behavior between the races (see Chapter 2 of this study). Her time in San Francisco in the early years of World War II allows Angelou to observe the slow disappearance of the Japanese as they are sent to internment camps, and the gradual occupation of the Japanese districts by African Americans. The experience of the Japanese and the job discrimination she herself faces teach her that southern whites are not the only ones who practice racism.

Scenes in the work are often dramatic, sometimes comic, and always carefully wrought with a lyrical but honest quality. When an interviewer suggests that writing a novel would be easy for An-gelou, Angelou's response confirms her preference for autobiog-raphy and again emphasizes her desire to tell the truth and her effort to convey a sense of collective experience: "I'm using the first-person singular, and trying to make that the first-person plu-ral, so that anybody can read the work and say, 'Hmm, that's the truth, yes, *uh-huh*,' and live in the work" (Angelou, "The Art of Fiction CXIX," 156). Indeed, Angelou often generalizes her expe-rience to provide insight into specific institutions, social settings, or characteristics and behaviors of a group or type. For example, at the conclusion of the opening scene, when she flees from church after her humiliating debacle in the Easter spectacle, An-gelou writes: "If growing up is painful for the Southern Black girl, being aware of her displacement is the rust on the razor that threatens the throat. It is an unnecessary insult" (3). Here she not only stresses her particular emotional devastation, but also extends her experience to relate it to the wider experience of the southern black girl.

But while Angelou's story embraces the larger issues, it is also the story of the kindness and love of particular people who had a positive effect on her life, and of the events that shaped and sometimes inspired her. In the second part of this analysis we will explore their impact.

SIGNIFICANT OTHERS AND EVENTS

From the age of three Maya is raised and nurtured by her strict and devoutly religious grandmother, whom she calls "Momma." Although Maya admits that she is often baffled by her grandmother's behavior, she clearly loves and respects her. This substitute mother-daughter relationship provides some security for the young Maya. Recent feminist studies emphasize the importance of the mother-daughter relationship for women's psychological development. Angelou gives prominence to the role of her grandmother (and later, her mother), and her narrative strategy bears witness to the impact these relationships had on her, and ultimately on her writing. For what is striking about her narrative choice is the importance she places on the role others have played in shaping her identity and destiny. Nancy Chodorow maintains that "because of their mothering by women, girls come to experience themselves as less separate than boys, as having more permeable ego boundaries. Girls come to define themselves more in relation to others" (93). In *A Poetics of Women's Autobiography*, Sidonie Smith reviews various theories of women's autobiography and cites among them "theories that distinguish women's autobiographies by the way in which women seem to unfold their story through their relationship to a significant 'other'" (18).[1]

There are several "significant others" in Angelou's narrative. Maya's deep feelings for her brother Bailey are an important lifeline for her. She depends on him for love, laughter, and wise counsel. Bailey's support is crucial in one of Maya's early experiences of racism. At the age of ten, Maya goes to work as a maid for a white woman, Viola Cullinan, who decides that Maya's given name,

Marguerite, is too long and arrogantly begins to call her Mary. Maya decides that she will not bear this indignity and that she must quit the job, but she knows that her grandmother will not allow her to quit without a good reason. Angelou credits Bailey with solving her dilemma. It is his idea that Maya break one of Mrs. Cullinan's favorite dishes in order to get herself fired. Bailey's idea works, and her success in carrying out this act, according to Sidonie Smith, "foreshadows Maya's eventual inability to sit quietly and is very much an expression of her growing acceptance of her own self-worth" (*Where I'm Bound*, 131).

It is also at the age of ten that Maya begins to move outside the family circle and finds a best friend, Louise Kendricks. After a good giggle over an impromptu game of looking into the sky and trying to fall into it, they become friends. According to Angelou, their time is spent playing jacks and hopscotch, and telling each other their deepest, darkest secrets. This description of her friendship with Louise is consistent with the observations of Carol Gilligan in her work about the psychosocial development of girls, *In a Different Voice*. According to Gilligan and the study by Janet Lever she cites, "girls' play tends to occur in smaller, more intimate groups, often the best-friend dyad, and in private places. . . . [I]t points less . . . toward learning to take the role of 'the generalized other,' less toward the abstraction of human relationships. But it fosters the development of the empathy and sensitivity necessary for taking the role of 'the particular other' " (11).

We have seen how Angelou valorizes the "particular other" among her family and friends and the significant role they play in providing Maya with security and affection. The role of another is again underscored as Angelou describes the mentors she credits with her intellectual development. During a yearlong stay with her real mother in St. Louis, Angelou is the victim of sexual assault at the age of seven, and as a result of the trauma involved with this incident, she stops talking. Upon her return to Stamps, Arkansas, Maya is invited to the home of her grandmother's friend, Bertha Flowers, who gently leads her back to speaking. Mrs. Flowers inspires in Maya a love for books and the beauty of the spoken word, and, most important, shows Maya that she can be liked just because of who she is. According to Smith, "it is Mrs. Flowers who opens the door to the caged bird's silence with the key of loving acceptance" (*Where I'm Bound*, 130).

Repeatedly Angelou expresses gratitude for the presence of "particular others" in her life and credits them for the person she becomes. But despite her attachment and gratitude to others, she is still trapped by the forces of sexism and racism. Her move to San Francisco during World War II to live with her mother is the first in a series of incidents that signal profound changes in Maya's life. The unsettled atmosphere that prevails in San Francisco during the war ironically frees Angelou from the persistent feeling of being an outsider. Later, while visiting her father, Angelou's self-confidence increases when, never having driven a car, she successfully negotiates her way down a Mexican mountain with her drunk father unconscious in the back seat. Smith sees this as a watershed event for Angelou: "For the first time, Maya finds herself totally in control of her situation. Her new sense of power contrasts vividly with her former despair that as a Negro she has no control over her fate" (*Where I'm Bound*, 132).

Another event during this visit with her father contributes to Maya's growing sense of well-being. After returning from the trip to Mexico, Angelou is stabbed by her father's jealous girlfriend, Dolores. Afraid to return home for fear of her mother's vengeful retribution upon Dolores, Angelou lives for a month in a junkyard with an assortment of other homeless children. This experience teaches Angelou respect for herself and others and furthers her sense of belonging.

It is during Maya's stay in San Francisco that her mother, Vivian Baxter, becomes a significant force in her life. Vivian's own determination and independence are qualities Maya emulates in her quest to be the first African American to be employed as a conductorette on the San Francisco cable cars. When Maya makes her decision to go to work, she reasons that her mother will support her because her mother believes in self-reliance and will appreciate her daughter's spunk. When Maya discovers that the cable car company will not hire African Americans, she stubbornly persists, haunting the streetcar office until she is hired. Sidonie Smith sees an important connection between the earlier episode with Mrs. Cullinan and Maya's rebellion against job discrimination: "Mrs. Cullinan's broken dish prefigures the job on the streetcar. . . . Maya assumes control over her own social destiny and engages in the struggle with life's forces. She has broken out of the rusted bars of her social cage" ("Song of a Caged Bird," 373).

The final step in the young Maya's journey to maturity and self-confidence occurs when she becomes pregnant. Suspicious that she may be a lesbian, Maya decides that she needs a boyfriend in order to assure herself about her sexual identity. To carry out her plan, Maya deliberately seduces a boy, and the result is an unplanned pregnancy. Her son is born when she is just sixteen years old, and for the first three weeks she is afraid to touch her child for fear that she may drop him or inflict some other injury on him. Finally, Maya's mother takes charge. Despite Maya's protests, Vivian insists that the baby sleep with Maya. Later in the night Vivian wakes her daughter up to show her that not only has she not crushed her son in her sleep, but she has intuitively protected her child while sleeping. Vivian's final lesson concludes *I Know Why the Caged Bird Sings*: "If you're for the right thing, then you do it without thinking" (246). This closing suggests that Maya's life has been a process of learning to value herself, of learning to trust her own strength, her intelligence, and her moral integrity. It is these qualities and the love and acceptance of her family, friends, and mentors that have enabled her to survive the personal defeats and the pain of oppression portrayed in *I Know Why the Caged Bird Sings*, and that will sustain her through future trials described in subsequent volumes of her autobiography.

But it is well to remember at this point Angelou's statement that her autobiography is more than just an account of her personal failures and triumphs. In his analysis, Cudjoe maintains that Angelou succeeds in being broadly representative of the experience of African Americans in her autobiographical works:

> As a statement, Angelou presents a powerful, authentic, and profound signification of Afro-American life and the changing concerns of the Afro-American woman in her quest for personal autonomy, understanding, and love. Such a statement, because of the simple, forthright, and honest manner in which it is presented, is depicted against the larger struggle of Afro-American and African peoples for their liberation and triumphs. It is a celebration of the struggle, survival, and existence of Afro-American people. (285)

Through her sensitive portrayal of the social environments and institutions that shaped her experience, Angelou achieves her objective of conveying the influence of the time period on her life and the lives of others. Angelou's autobiography succeeds, then, on two levels: first, as a personal memoir of a single individual who was able to survive; and second, as a representative narrative that exemplifies the struggle of many African American women against racial and sexual oppression.

NOTES

1. See my article "Simone de Beauvoir and Maya Angelou: Birds of a Feather," in *Simone de Beauvoir Studies*, 6 (1989), in which I quote this same passage and which served as the starting point for this chapter.

STUDY QUESTIONS

1. Why has autobiography been such an important genre in the African American literary tradition?

2. What are some of the dominant themes in black women's autobiography?

3. Why is the question of truth in an autobiography a complex issue?

4. What are Angelou's stated intentions in writing her autobiography? Do you think she achieves her goals?

5. Consider what impact Angelou's point of view as a mature adult has on how she chooses to tell her story.

6. Consider the importance of the opening scene. What themes introduced in this scene are repeated throughout the autobiography?

7. To what extent are the environment and time period in which her life story takes place important?

8. How would you characterize Angelou's style—her language, her tone, her choice of metaphors, and so on?

9. Who are the people who contributed to Angelou's survival? How did they contribute?

10. What events helped Angelou to feel that she had a place where she belonged and led her to feel increased tolerance for people different from herself?

11. How does the conclusion of the autobiography contribute a sense of closure to the story?

TOPICS FOR WRITTEN OR ORAL EXPLORATION

1. Read Paul Laurence Dunbar's poem "Sympathy" and show how the themes of the poem relate to the themes of Angelou's autobiography and its title.

2. Discuss the significance of the symbol of the cage in the autobiography.

3. Compare and contrast Mrs. Flowers and Momma.

4. Where do we see evidence of Angelou's strength and determination to resist oppression?

5. In your opinion, what does it mean to write "an autobiography as literature"? Does Angelou succeed in doing so?

6. To what extent and in what specific instances in her autobiography

are Angelou's experiences connected to the experiences of African Americans in general?

7. Read subsequent volumes of Angelou's autobiography. What aspects of her character and/or experience as described in *I Know Why the Caged Bird Sings* are significant for her in later years?

8. Compare Angelou's *I Know Why the Caged Bird Sings* to Richard Wright's *Black Boy* and/or Anne Moody's *Coming of Age in Mississippi*. What similarities and differences do you see in their stories and their narrative choices? Consider, for example, each author's representation of the Jim Crow era in the South and the degree to which others play a significant role in their lives.

WORKS CITED

Angelou, Maya. "The Art of Fiction CXIX: Maya Angelou." Interview with George Plimpton. *Paris Review* 32 (Fall 1990): 144–67.

———. *I Know Why the Caged Bird Sings*. 1970. Toronto: Bantam Books, 1971.

Chodorow, Nancy. *The Reproduction of Mothering*. Berkeley: University of California Press, 1978.

Conway, Jill Ker, ed. *Written by Herself: Autobiographies of American Women. An Anthology*. New York: Vintage, 1992.

Cudjoe, Selwyn R. "Maya Angelou: The Autobiographical Statement Updated." In *Reading Black, Reading Feminist: A Critical Anthology*. Ed. Henry Louis Gates, Jr. New York: Meridian, 1990. 272–306.

Gilligan, Carol. *In a Different Voice*. Cambridge, Mass.: Harvard University Press, 1982.

Megna-Wallace, Joanne. "Simone de Beauvoir and Maya Angelou: Birds of a Feather." *Simone de Beauvoir Studies* 6 (1989): 50–55.

Smith, Sidonie. *A Poetics of Women's Autobiography: Marginality and the Fictions of Self-Representation*. Bloomington: Indiana University Press, 1987.

———. "The Song of a Caged Bird: Maya Angelou's Quest after Self-Acceptance." *Southern Humanities Review* (Fall 1973): 365–75.

———. *Where I'm Bound: Patterns of Slavery and Freedom in Black American Autobiography*. Westport, Conn.: Greenwood Press, 1974.

Tate, Claudia, ed. *Black Women Writers at Work*. New York: Continuum, 1983.

SUGGESTED READINGS

Abel, Elizabeth, Marianne Hirsch, and Elizabeth Langland, eds. *The Voyage In: Fictions of Female Development*. Hanover, N.H.: University Press of New England, 1983.

Braxton, Joanne M. *Black Women Writing Autobiography: A Tradition Within a Tradition*. Philadelphia: Temple University Press, 1989. (See in particular the introduction and chapter 6: "A Song of Transcendence: Maya Angelou".)

Elliot, Jeffrey M., ed. *Conversations with Maya Angelou*. Jackson: University Press of Mississippi, 1989.

Gates, Henry Louis, Jr., ed. *Reading Black, Reading Feminist: A Critical Anthology*. New York: Meridian, 1990.

Jelinek, Estelle, ed. *Women's Autobiography: Essays in Criticism*. Bloomington: Indiana University Press, 1980.

Kent, George E. "Maya Angelou's *I Know Why the Caged Bird Sings* and Black Autobiographical Tradition." *Kansas Quarterly* 7, 3 (1975): 72–78.

Stanton, Domna C. *The Female Autograph: Theory and Practice of Autobiography from the Tenth to the Twentieth Century*. Chicago: University of Chicago Press, 1987.

2

Violence and Intimidation as a Means of Social Control: A Historical Overview of Race Relations in the South

Maya Angelou's portrayal of her childhood in Stamps, Arkansas, contains many episodes that provide important insights into race relations in the South in the 1930s. Segregation was a deeply ingrained part of southern culture and governed all aspects of social interaction. Many jobs were not open to African Americans, and they typically held only the lowest paid jobs. Blacks and whites lived in different parts of town, with African Americans relegated to the poorer areas. The two races went to different hospitals, were usually limited to treatment by doctors and dentists of their own race, attended separate schools and churches, used separate public restroom facilities and drinking fountains, swam at different beaches, ate in different restaurants, shopped at different establishments, and occupied different areas of movie theatres, with African Americans confined to the balconies only. Similarly, blacks and whites sat in different areas on buses, and African Americans were forced to sit in the back. If there was a shortage of seats, an African American was obliged to yield his or her seat to a white customer.

Laws sanctioning the legal separation of blacks and whites, the so-called Jim Crow laws, originated with legislation regulating train travel. The following excerpt is from an 1891 Arkansas law, "An Act to Promote the Comfort of Passengers on Railways and Other Purposes":

Be it enacted by the General Assembly of the State of Arkansas:
Section 1. That all railway companies carrying passengers in their
coaches in this State shall provide equal but separate and sufficient
accommodations for the white and African races, by providing two
or more passenger coaches for each passenger train. *Provided*, That
on all lines of railway less then [*sic*] twenty-five miles long, passenger coaches may be divided by a partition so as to secure separate
accommodations, and they shall also provide separate waiting-
rooms of equal and sufficient accommodation for the two races at
all their passenger depots in this State. (Boyd, 9)

This type of legislation was common in southern states, and
other Jim Crow laws quickly followed, regulating every conceivable
type of social interaction. In *Jim Crow Guide to the U.S.A.*, Stetson
Kennedy provides the following summary of some of the laws in
Arkansas regarding sexual relations that reveals the extreme
lengths to which lawmakers went in order to discourage or prohibit interracial marriage or cohabitation:

A person having any Negro blood may not engage in concubinage
with a white, but may marry a white *provided* the Negro blood is
not "visible and distinct."
"Concubinage between a person of the Caucasian or white race
and between a person of the negro or black race is hereby made a
felony."
Penalty: One month to one year "at hard labor" for each offence.
Court rulings: "Living together or cohabitation, whether open or
secret," is contrary to law. However, "occasional intercourse" does
not constitute concubinage or cohabitation. "No person shall be
convicted of the crime of concubinage upon the testimony of the
female, unless the same is corroborated by other evidence."
Childbearing: "Any woman who shall have been delivered of a
mulatto child, the same shall be *prima facie* evidence of guilt without further proof and shall justify a conviction of the woman." It is
the duty of magistrates to issue warrants in such cases in the name
of the state, and to prosecute. No *Negro* mother of a mulatto child
has ever been prosecuted under this law. (Kennedy, 64)

These and other Jim Crow laws were quite effective in ensuring
the separation of blacks and whites. Angelou declares that in
Stamps, segregation was so thorough that she was unsure whether
whites were real; a trip to the white part of town felt like she was

"walking without weapons into man-eating animals' territory" (*Caged Bird*, 20). Segregation was enforced through the constant threat of physical violence and intimidation by whites against blacks. When Bailey comes home late one evening, past his curfew, Momma is not merely angry at a disobedient child; she fears that he has been the victim of a lynching. When Bailey stumbles on the corpse of a black man who has just been pulled from the pond, his genitals cut off, he witnesses the hatred of a white man who is delighted over the death of this black man, in fact, any black man.

The heartless refusal of a white dentist to treat Maya because of her race further contributes to her understanding of what can be expected from white folks. When her white employer, Mrs. Cullinan, shortens her name from Marguerite to Mary for the sake of her own convenience, Maya experiences firsthand the prevailing white attitude of superiority over blacks. Finally, the psychological impact of racism is represented in Maya's own internalized racism when she dreams of waking up, happily transformed into a beautiful white girl.

Maya's lessons on racial etiquette, the expectations governing social interactions between the two races, are learned from her grandmother. In a culture where violence was an acceptable means of keeping African Americans "in their place," where the justice system and law enforcement officials failed to protect them and might even condone or participate in violent attacks against them, safety was of paramount importance: "Momma intended to teach Bailey and me to use the paths of life that she and her generation and all the Negroes gone before had found, and found to be safe ones. She didn't cotton to the idea that white-folks could be talked to at all without risking one's life. And certainly they couldn't be spoken to insolently" (39).

The documents in this chapter provide a historical context for Angelou's presentation of her encounters with the physical and psychological violence of racism. They demonstrate the range of violent methods used to oppress African Americans, from the enforced servitude of slavery, to the threat and reality of lynchings and other forms of physical intimidation after Emancipation, to the economic and social inequality created by racism. Included are excerpts from a scholarly essay that gives a general historical overview of violence against African Americans during and since slavery; excerpts from a study on lynching published by the

Commission on Interracial Cooperation; newspaper articles documenting two lynchings in Arkansas during the 1930s; and, finally, an interview that discusses the expectations and taboos of racial etiquette and the accommodation attitudes developed by African Americans in response to racism.

HISTORICAL OVERVIEW OF RACE RELATIONS

The following essay provides an analysis of the history of white violence against blacks, the methods employed to dominate African Americans during slavery, through Reconstruction and into the twentieth century, and the response of African Americans to these methods of social control. James Comer, an assistant professor of psychiatry at the Yale Child Study Center when he wrote this piece, was uniquely qualified to explore the psychological impact of violence against African Americans, for adults as well as children. Comer's insights into the socialization of children in a violent environment are particularly relevant for an understanding of Angelou's childhood and psychological development.

Comer deplores the harmful effects of physical and social violence for groups and individuals and poses the question at the heart of his analysis: Why have African Americans not resisted sooner and more forcefully the violence to which they have been subjected throughout U.S. history? He begins with a historical overview, detailing methods of violence during slavery and following Emancipation. He then explores the methods of socialization that assured that slaves remained powerless. These methods included legal, cultural, and psychological means. Although legally free after 1865, the legacy of slavery remained with blacks, most of whom were still economically, socially, and psychologically dependent on whites. Poor educational opportunities, severely limited employment options, and segregation, as well as white violence and intimidation, all worked to keep blacks in an inferior social position and to persuade many that they were indeed inferior.

It is this atmosphere of deprivation and violence that prevails in *I Know Why the Caged Bird Sings*. Although Maya's grandmother owns her own store and some land, it is clear that Maya's family and the African Americans in her community struggle to survive economically. The threat of violence is ever present and keenly felt by the young Maya in her encounters with whites. Maya observes her fellow African Americans' response to the violence and intimidation—their necessary accommodations to racism—and her story is testimony to the sense of powerlessness and inferiority that may result and that must be vigorously opposed.

JAMES P. COMER, M.D., "THE DYNAMICS OF BLACK AND WHITE
VIOLENCE," IN HUGH GRAHAM, AND TED ROBERT GURR,
*VIOLENCE IN AMERICA: HISTORICAL AND COMPARATIVE
PERSPECTIVES.* VOLUME 2.
(Washington, D.C.: National Commission on the Causes and
Prevention of Violence, 1969)

It is the task of the leaders of a society to establish social policy that
facilitates optimal individual development and adequate socialization of
the young. Failure to do so constitutes social violence, resulting in damage to individuals, groups, and the society, which is far more harmful
and lasting than overt physical violence. In a representative society where
groups must organize and participate in the political and administrative
system in order to obtain opportunities that will facilitate the optimal
development of their members, the obstructive and unjust exercise of
power—physical or social—by another group constitutes a crippling
form of violence. The victimized group, when healthy, struggles against
the unjust and oppressive situation. This struggle in the face of resistance
frequently results in overt physical violence. In addition, when the leaders
of a society sanction social exploitation of a group, they concomitantly
encourage physical violence toward that group. Thus the historical American situation of slavery or legal social violence toward blacks; white physical violence and relatively little black retaliation. . . .

There is an aspect of the pattern—black restraint—which, on the surface, is difficult to explain. Given the level of social violence toward
blacks, the logical question now should not be "Why black violence?"
but "Why has black initiated and retaliatory violence been so little and
so late?" The record of provocation certainly is extreme.

During slavery, whippings and other abusive acts were frequent. Because of the economic value of the slave, it was usually only after abortive
slave revolts or "unpardonable" offences that the killing of slaves took
place. Freedmen, North and South, who found themselves in economic
competition with whites frequently fared less well. After slavery when the
4 million blacks in the South came into direct economic competition with
the 5–1/2 million poor whites and were no longer of value to the white
planters, the severity of violence toward blacks increased. Beatings, torture, and murder in order to disfranchise blacks, decrease economic competition, and maintain a caste system for economic and psychological
advantage became the pattern of the day. It has been estimated that between 1865 and 1955 over 5,000 blacks were lynched by white mobs.
Official U.S. Census Bureau statistics show that over 3,000 were lynched

between 1882 and 1935. Legal lynchings, "kangaroo court" action, and unreported murders are not included in these totals. Black schools and homes were frequently burned in the postslavery period. Between 1865 and 1940, over 500 blacks were killed in race riots and massacres. Many more were injured and abused. Relatively few whites were killed in these disturbances. . . .

Despite this abusive and oppressive pattern, black reaction was generally not violence but nonviolence. Aptheker and other historians have pointed out that there were slave uprisings and rumors of uprisings, but they certainly did not approximate the frequency or severity of black slave uprisings in South America. Even after slavery there was generally an under response to the level of oppression. Historians and revolutionaries have often puzzled over and despaired about this situation.

Certainly the overwhelming power of the dominant group is a factor. But it is not enough to explain the phenomenon. Often slaves and freedmen greatly outnumbered their masters and sometimes did attack and kill them, but not very often. Subsequent events have demonstrated that inherent docility and passivity and the other explanations for extreme black restraint were inaccurate. This is evidenced by the remarkable change in black reaction to white control efforts in a short period of time. Only 15 years ago a black family stood fearful and powerless as whites, without legal authority, dragged their black youngster from his home and murdered him. Today the arrest of a black man by a white policeman in a black neighborhood carries with it the risk of touching off a violent disturbance. Obviously there are important psychosocial forces at play in black and white violence which go beyond simple unhappiness and re-action to racism or poverty. These forces can best be delineated through a review of the critical aspects of black and white reaction over time.

Slavery, the initial contact of most blacks and whites in America, set the stage for continuing conflict. . . .

The objective of socialization in slavery was not to develop the individual to a point that he or she might perform as a fully adequate, competent, full participant in adult society. The socialization and management of slaves was designed to maintain the master's power and control over them and to increase his benefits. Even humane treatment had its "master's twist." An ex-slave from Louisiana said, "Marse always say being mean to the young-uns make them mean when they grows up and nobody gwine to buy a mean nigger."

The slaves were powerless for two major reasons. Their legal status was that of chattel without rights in court and without the protection of any institution. The master was all-powerful and had the right to control every aspect of slave life from birth to death, from sex to settling disputes. His power was enhanced by additional factors. Black slaves in a predominantly white controlled land were readily identifiable. The slaves were not of a single tribal origin with a long group history and a resultant cohesive bond. They were far from home and generally unwanted except for economic exploitation. They were not able to maintain the organizational elements of their respective previous cultures—kinship ties, family organization, religion, government, courts, etc. Thus they were not able to run away en masse; to turn in on their own culture for psychological support or to effectively organize to attack their oppressors. . . .

After the first generation, children were born into the system and prepared from birth for a life of subservience. Nurturance and physical care came from an adult but not in the interest of a family, kinship group, or tribe, but in the interest of a master. . . .

Children were taught what they could and could not do in relation to whites. They were taught to obey and respect whites. The Bible and the whip reinforced their parent's teaching. Frequent references in the literature of slavery indicate that black children were taught to knuckle under to the little white tyrant of the same age, one in training to become the master and the other to become the slave. There could be no black-group goals for children to inculcate. Blacks did not exist as a group with goals of their own. They were given organization, goals and direction by the master. They existed for his benefit and by his permission. . . .

It is understandable under the condition of powerlessness, dependency and rejection inherent in the nature of American slavery that wisdom and adequacy became associated with the master. Eventually these attributes were extended to all white persons. All whites had the right to abuse and exploit blacks without fear of serious censure or consequences. Blackness was associated with inadequacy and subservience and the notion was transmitted to black and white children during their earliest developmental years. . . .

Identification with the master was of serious psychological consequence to the slaves. Attitudes about blacks held by whites became the feelings or attitudes blacks held for themselves and each other as a group. Hatred of self, anger toward the self, presumption of black incompetence, etc., are a legacy of slavery reinforced by residual and later social practices—segregation and exclusion. . . .

After slavery, blacks were immediately closed out of the economic, political, and educational mainstream of American life. The program of federal Reconstruction failed to provide blacks with a solid economic base and was, as a consequence, gradually eroded as an adjustment tool. None of the organizational aspects of the African culture remained to provide a basis for group stability and direction. Only remnants of previous African life styles and behavioral residuals remained, greatly modified by the American experience and of little value in promoting adjustment in the postslavery period. As a result of these factors, blacks remained economically, socially, and psychologically dependent on whites who retained almost complete economic and social control. Over 50 percent of the black population remained in a condition of serfdom until the early part of the 20th century. While some were able to directly express anger and advocate rejection of and attacks on the perceived oppressor—as some did in slavery—most were not able to do so. Not only had their training been effective but to express hostility toward whites on which many were dependent was to risk the loss of a major source of a sense of security.

The circumstances reflected an extremely unhealthy state of affairs. As a group, blacks were unable to obtain opportunities which would facilitate the optimal development of large numbers of their members. Public education was long delayed and often inadequate. They were employed at the lowest level of the job market. They were rapidly closed out of business and government. Yet because many had been trained to accept white control, their lack of education and skills, the level of antagonism toward blacks, and their dependency tie to whites with power, many blacks—although woefully oppressed—were unable to struggle against the unjust exercise of power they experienced. This combination of circumstances did not exist for any other excluded group in America.

Although powerless after slavery with still little sense of community other than being a despised, rejected part of a larger community, blacks were forced to turn in on themselves anyway. Segregation, which rapidly developed as a social policy after slavery, made this necessary. With the end of the control and exploitation of blacks by their masters, legislation, judicial and extra-legal control (intimidation, violence, economic reprisals) were established. Control and authority had now been extended to all whites, most of them more economically vulnerable and in need of psychological scapegoats than the more wealthy slaveowning class. Whites outside the planter class were more likely to act in an unjust and violent fashion toward blacks. Black parents had to prepare their children to live in such a setting. Aggressive styles had to be crushed lest they lead to conflicts with whites. Such socialization led to the destruction and/or diminution of the capacity for exploration, learning, and work in many blacks.

A strict social etiquette developed which symbolized white privilege and black subservience. Children learned the rules of the game through subtle and overt ways. In the 1930's when a black youngster in Texas was beaten by white adult males for entering a bus before a white woman, his father did not protect or console him but angrily counseled, "You ought to know better than to get on the bus before the white folks."

The implication of segregation, as it was practiced, was clear: blacks are inferior and incapable of participation in the total society. . . .

The circumstances of black and white interaction [have] also had an impact on the white psyche. Until recent years, many whites have felt justified in their abuse and exploitation of blacks. Leaders of the society—a U.S. Congressman as late as the early 1900's—threatened greater violence toward blacks if favorable legislation for them was passed. During Reconstruction, many white leaders urged the white masses to attack blacks and often joined in the fun. It is small wonder that a cavalier attitude (indeed a collective superego defect) developed with regard to white abuse of black. It was wrong to murder unless it was a nigger out of his place—his place being determined by whites.

Inherent superiority was taught and is still taught to white youngsters through denial and by ignoring the accomplishments of blacks in the face of overwhelming obstacles. Institutional denial—exclusion of blacks from textbooks, communications media, and white institutions—facilitated individual denial. . . . These attitudes and conditions are clearly changing under the pressure of new social forces, but many undesirable conditions still exist. Such attitudes and reactions are, in part, a basis for continued black and white conflict. (343–50)

LYNCHING AS A METHOD OF
SOCIAL CONTROL

Early in *I Know Why the Caged Bird Sings*, Angelou recounts an incident in which her family is warned that there may be an attempted lynching that night and that her Uncle Willie could be a target. She describes her fear when a former sheriff rides in and announces to her grandmother: "Annie, tell Willie he better lay low tonight. A crazy nigger messed with a white lady today. Some of the boys'll be coming over here later" (14).

Although estimates vary, statistics indicate that lynching was a widespread phenomenon after Reconstruction and during the first third of the twentieth century, particularly in the South, and that African Americans were by far the most frequent victims of lynching. In *A Festival of Violence: An Analysis of Southern Lynchings, 1882–1930*, Tolnay and Beck estimate that during the five decades between the end of Reconstruction and the beginning of the Great Depression "there were 2,018 separate incidents of lynching in which at least 2,462 African American men, women, and children met their deaths in the grasp of southern mobs, comprised mostly of whites" (17). *Lynchings and What They Mean* provides these statistics for specific states, including Arkansas: "Since 1889 Mississippi, Georgia, Texas, and Louisiana have had the largest numbers of lynchings, with 465, 464, 364, and 349 respectively. However, the lynching rate per ten thousand Negro population is considerably higher for Florida, Oklahoma, and Arkansas than for either of the four states mentioned. . . . Florida, with its phenomenal population growth in recent decades, shows a lynching rate of 4.5 per ten thousand Negro population during the 1900–1930 period. . . . Other Southern States where the Negro's life has been least secure from the mob include Oklahoma, with a rate of 3.9; Arkansas, 2.9; and Texas, 2.5" (8–10, 13).

Tolnay and Beck theorize that lynchings as a method of social control became necessary only after Emancipation, as slavery had successfully controlled African Americans prior to the Civil War. But with freedom for African Americans came the threat of competition for political and economic power previously enjoyed exclusively by whites. "Whites saw nearly four million southern blacks suddenly transformed from personal property to potential competitors" (57). These authors argue that whites believed it was necessary to neutralize the economic threat posed by African Americans and that the following methods were devised: "Jim Crow legislation, disenfranchisement, judicial discrimination, debt peonage, and violent intimidation were included in the repertory of social control techniques. It is within this context that mob violence can be viewed as an instrument of social control over a 'threatening' southern black population" (57).

The Commission on Interracial Cooperation expanded on these themes in *The Mob Still Rides*, tying lynching to racial exploitation. The document details the economic, political, and cultural manifestations of racial exploitation and articulates the view that lynching was only the most extreme method of keeping African Americans in their place. In *I Know Why the Caged Bird Sings* one sees the traumatic fear and humiliation the threat of lynching inspires, and one understands that to resist the racial status quo was to risk death. The document also provides a profile of the possible motivations for the perpetrators of lynchings, often poorer rural whites who needed to believe that another group of people was inferior to them to assure themselves of their own superiority.

The Mob Still Rides also addresses the role of law enforcement officers in lynchings, noting that "lynchers go unpunished because punishment of their crime depends upon the same peace officers and court officials whose impotence they demonstrated when they lynched; the officers of the law have already shown their unwillingness or inability to administer justice; and lynchers, in most cases, are responsible only to the local courts" (11). Furthermore, not a few officers cooperate in the lynchings, in some instances conniving, in others participating" (12).

THE MOB STILL RIDES: A REVIEW OF THE LYNCHING RECORD, 1931–1935
(Atlanta: Commission on Interracial Cooperation, 1936)

Lynching and Racial Exploitation

With most lynchings occurring in the South and the Negro, "America's tenth man," furnishing ninety per cent of the victims in recent years, one logically looks to the Southern racial situation for the underlying causes of lynchings. Formerly an instrument of popular justice in frontier communities, and still retaining something of its frontier character, lynching and the threat of it are now primarily a technique of enforcing racial exploitation—economic, political, and cultural.

Economic exploitation of the Negro by the American white man is as old and as continuous as the Negro's presence on American soil. Slavery, peonage, low wages, restricted work opportunities, and inferior educational and other public welfare facilities record his principal economic handicaps in the developing American scene.

The exploitation of the Negro extends from its broad economic base into all the vital phases of political life. State, county, and municipal governments—the legal instruments of the whites—secure more money for white schools by diverting to them a portion of the public monies which belong to the Negro. For much the same reason the Negro has poorer public health service, poorer police protection, and frequently a smaller pauper allowance or relief order. He seldom sits on a jury, and almost never has a voice in the allocation of public funds.

Most insidious of all has been the cultural exploitation of the Negro. The typical popular story, from political platform and pulpit, commonly represents him as an amiable simpleton, lacking in morals, intelligence, and ambition. Black-faced characters are good drawing cards for white audiences, perhaps because white people like to see Negroes dependent and docile, and in ridiculous roles. All this rests on certain rationalizations, chief of which is the assumption that the Negro has been ordained to a position of subservience and servitude. Thus his political impotence and economic helplessness are enforced.

The exploitation of the black folk has been something of a profession. Many business men and politicians have capitalized [on] race prejudice to gain larger profits through lower labor costs or to make their political and institutional leadership secure. The South's Watsons, Bleases, Heflins, and Vardamans in politics and other fields have not been mental dwarfs. They saw a harvest for themselves and reaped it. The success of the professional Negro-phobe has rested in no small degree upon conditions which he has been instrumental in creating and maintaining.

In most communities of the South the role of the Negro is rigorously defined. He has the poorer schools and a disproportionate share of illiteracy, fewer public health nurses and greater morbidity, fewer parks and a higher juvenile delinquency rate, smaller houses and more unmarried mothers, limited employment and longer bread lines, longer hours, smaller wages, and a higher death rate. The whites who thus define "his place" insist that he stay in it and promptly suppress any revolt against his economic dependence, political impotence, and cultural subservience.

The whole spotted fabric of lynching has one thread running through it: The Negro must be kept in his place. Lynchings and threats of violence are but the more extreme expressions of the white man's determination to continue his exploitation of the Negro, which is most thorough when the Negro knows that he chooses between subservience and annihilation. Rural whites may point out that it is about time for another lynching when they think the Negro no longer fears one.

To understand why the mob emerges most often in the rural Southern community with a low economic and cultural rank, it is well to remember that exploitation, prevalent in practically all communities, is often carried out by cruder methods in poorer communities than in richer ones. To maintain their control over Negro labor, the leading white people lynch in some communities. But it is the poorer rural whites, who live on about the same plane as the landless Negroes near-by, to whom man hunts, mock trials and lynchings prove most attractive. The racial dogma is precious to them because it is proof that they are superior. They find a welcomed reassurance in the color of their skins and the license it affords. Momentarily they escape the boredom of their restricted lives; for a time they are people of importance—they assume the role of society's protectors; they flourish weapons; they hunt down the accused; they determine his guilt; they destroy him, sometimes with protracted torture. In reality, lynchings come out of the state of mind of white people much more than out of the crimes committed by Negroes, just as witches were burned in Boston, not because there were witches in Boston but because of the state of mind of the people in Boston.

So Negroes are lynched, some accused of capital crimes, others of little or nothing. Most of the victims are hanged and then riddled with bullets, some are dismembered or burned; some of the bodies are removed at once, others are left as gory spectacles for men, women, and children to view—a topic of conversation in shop, sewing circle, and home. And native-born white lynchers, some with property and more with none, are seldom indicted and almost never convicted. (23–24)

TWO ACCOUNTS OF LYNCHINGS FROM THE *ARKANSAS GAZETTE*

The newspaper articles included here document two lynchings that took place in Arkansas during the period about which Angelou writes. In the first incident, the African American male who is lynched is accused of the same crime that allegedly had occurred the day Maya's Uncle Willie is warned that he must hide or face the wrath of a vengeful mob. In addition, it is important to note that no one in the mob can be identified even though the victim was taken directly from the custody of the city marshal. Finally, no charges had been filed against the African American man, although the alleged assault was said to have occurred eleven days before the lynching.

"YOUNG NEGRO LYNCHED AT LEPANTO"
(Arkansas Gazette [Little Rock], April 30, 1936: 1)

Lepanto, Ark., April 29 (AP)—A 19-year-old Negro accused of an attempted attack on a white woman here April 18, was taken from the city marshal early today by a crowd of masked men and shot to death.

The Negro, Willie Kees, was found at the edge of town with his hands bound behind his back and three bullet wounds in the body. One shot pierced the heart.

Deputy Sheriff Mert Walker said that Kees was accused of the attempted assault and ordered to leave town several days ago. He returned Monday, and was arrested by City Marshal Jay May this morning. On the way to jail the mob appeared.

May said they overpowered him, forced the Negro into an automobile and sped away. When the victim was found, he had a bullet through his heart, another in his back and a third in his left leg. No one was near the body when he was found.

The lynching was the first to occur in Poinsctt county.

"None of Mob Recognized"

Deputy Walker said officers had been unable to identify any of the mob as they wore masks and that Kees was warned to leave town after Marshal May saved him from one mob that "set out to bump him off."

Walker said the marshal arrested the Negro the night of the attempted assault on the woman.

"She was attacked on the bridge at the edge of town," he said, "but she screamed and two men ran up and saved her. The Negro was turned over to the marshal and placed in jail.

"That night May heard that a mob was coming to get him but he met them and talked them out of it. It was dark and he couldn't recognize any of them.

"The next morning early he told Kees he would release him if the Negro would leave the county and not return. No charges had been filed against the Negro."

"Deny Negro Was Whipped"

Marshal May verified Walker's version of Kees' release, both denying a report that the Negro was whipped before he was ordered to leave the county.

"After I turned him loose," May said, "I heard that he was staying at the home of another Negro about a half mile from town and that a mob was going to get him.

"I went to the house and arrested him and was bringing him back to jail when the mob of about 10 men drove up in two cars, right at the place where he tried to attack the woman."

The marshal said the men wore burlap sacks over their heads and were armed. Seven of them held guns on him, while three others took the Negro and forced him into a car. They drove through Lepanto, the marshal said, and two hours later the Negro's body was found at the edge of town.

May said there had been no action by authorities to attempt to identify members of the mob, because he had been unable to recognize any of them.

He described the young Negro as "half-witted" and said he had been arrested several times before on theft charges.

"NEGRO LYNCHED BY MOB AT CROSSETT"
(*Arkansas Gazette* [Little Rock], September 16, 1932, 1)

Crossett, Sept. 15.—Frank Tucker, Negro, aged 24, was hanged by a mob of approximately 500 persons in the Ashley county jail yard here shortly after 6 tonight after the Negro had attacked Deputy City Marshal Henry Reed, 45, and slashed his throat with a razor. The officer was in a serious condition at a Crossett hospital tonight.

Tucker was under arrest in connection with the theft of 10 silver dollars from the Bank of Crossett. He was being held in the office of Mayor I.M. Barnes with another Negro, Tommy Wells, also a suspect in the theft. Officer Reed was seated on a chair between the two.

Presently Tucker arose, stepped toward Marshal Reed and demanded that the officer hand over his pistol. As the officer turned to face the Negro, Tucker slashed him with a razor. The Negro had been searched, but no weapons had been found.

Tucker then ran out the front door. Several persons on the street started in pursuit. The crowd grew rapidly. Tucker was captured about four blocks from the mayor's office.

"Led Through Business District"

A rope was tied around the Negro's neck. He was led through the business section of Crossett and to the yard of the Ashley county jail. Hundreds of persons witnessed the spectacle. There were approximately 500 persons in the jail yard when the lynching occurred. One end of the rope was thrown over an iron pipe within 12 inches of the jail, and the Negro was hoisted about 20 or 25 feet from the ground.

The body was left dangling to the end of the rope 46 minutes, until Sheriff John Riley arrived and cut it down. The sheriff was out of town when the lynching took place.

Soon after Sheriff Riley cut the body down, the crowd began to disperse, and within an hour or two the city presented a normal appearance.

The mayor's office, where the attack of the officer occurred, is in the center of the business section and directly across the street from the postoffice.

This was said to have been the first lynching in Crossett.

The scene of the lynching was about 300 yards from the home of the victim's father. The body was taken there after it was cut down. No coroner's investigation had been conducted tonight. Neither had there been any arrests.

The condition of Marshal Reed was said at the hospital tonight to be critical. The jugular vein was severed, but the razor blade did not touch the artery. Opiates were administered soon after he reached the hospital, and late tonight attendants said he was resting comfortably.

Marshal Reed has lived in Crossett about eight years, and has been a peace officer three years. He is well and favorably known among the business men of the city. He has a wife and two sons.

Tucker had lived here practically all his life. He was a lumber mill employe. Officers said tonight he never had been in serious trouble before.

RACIAL ETIQUETTE AND ACCOMMODATION ATTITUDES

In *The Negro Personality: A Rigorous Investigation of the Effects of Culture* Bertram P. Karon observes that the racial etiquette governing "all" contacts between Negroes and whites in the South is an elaborate ceremonious code which renders these interracial contacts as impersonal as possible" (18). David Goldfield provides the following examples of the racial etiquette in *Black, White, and Southern: Race Relations and Southern Culture, 1940 to the Present*: "For blacks encountering whites, the code demanded, among other things, 'sir' and 'ma'am,' averted eyes, preferably a smile, never imparting bad news, never discussing other whites, and always exhibiting a demeanor that would make a white comfortable in believing that this deferential mien was not only right but the way things ought to be" (2).

One of Maya's experiences with the racial etiquette is described when her grandmother's store is visited by a group of what she calls powhitetrash children. Angelou portrays her shame at her powerlessness to prevent the humiliations inflicted by the white children who presume to call her grandmother by her first name and who dare to mock her. And she is enraged that her grandmother addresses the offenders with the title "Miz."

Karon's analysis suggests that Maya's grandmother was responding to the social expectations demanded in black-white interactions:

> Recognition of the inferiority of the Negro is embodied in the ritual of face-to-face discussions by the use of distinctions in the forms of address. The Negro is expected always to show his respect by using the title Mr., Mrs., or Miss when talking to a white person, while the white person addresses the Negro by the latter's first name, irrespective of how little acquaintance the two may have, or by the condescending epithet "boy" and its alternatives "uncle," "auntie," "elder," etc. These are used with no regard to the age of the Negro being addressed. . . . It is clear that this etiquette is designed to demonstrate that the Negro is inferior *and* that he recognizes it in the sense that he is willing to act out the ritual. (Of course, he has no real alternative.) (20–21)

When Maya dares to believe she has an alternative to the racial status quo and challenges the racial etiquette upon her return to Stamps in the second volume of her autobiography, *Gather Together in My Name*, her grandmother promptly and forcefully impresses upon her the rashness of her actions. In this episode, Maya talks back to two clerks at the general store in the white part of town. Her grandmother receives a phone call and is waiting for Maya when she triumphantly returns. When Maya tries to explain, she is repeatedly slapped by her grandmother, who tells her: "You think 'cause you've been to California these crazy people won't kill you? You think them lunatic cracker boys won't try to catch you in the road and violate you? You think because of your all-fired principle some of the men won't feel like putting their white sheets on and riding over here to stir up trouble? You do, you're wrong. Ain't nothing to protect you and us except the good Lord and some miles" (93). With no further discussion, Maya is packed off to her mother in San Francisco.

Maya's grandmother's caution was typical of the attitude of many African Americans who had learned from firsthand experience and the experiences of others that conformity to expected behavior was a matter of life or death. As Goldfield notes:

> Prudence born of fear usually inhibited retaliation or departure from behavioral norms. Stories of white brutality against blacks, often for minor transgressions, circulated through black communities. As [Richard] Wright explained, "the things that influenced my conduct as a Negro did not have to happen to me directly. . . . Indeed the white brutality that I had not seen was a more effective control of my behavior than that which I knew." In 1955, Anne Moody, a black Mississippi teenager, heard news of a lynching near her Delta home. She recalled her immobilizing fear: "I didn't know what one had to do or not to do as a Negro not to be killed." So a constant tension gripped blacks in their relations with whites, an uneasiness that a wrong word or a gesture could have serious consequences (7).

The final document in this chapter is a 1939 interview with an African American that demonstrates the consequences of failing to observe the racial etiquette. Note that rather than attributing his child's death and his own thwarted ambitions to their real cause, white racism, Charlie Holcomb instead has come to believe that the place of African Americans has been decided by God and that his own race is inferior. His account and interpretation are an illustration of the accommodation attitude adopted by many African Americans, as described in *Caste and Class in a Southern Town*: "Accommodation attitudes are those which enable the Negro to adjust and survive in the caste situation as it is presented to him. . . . Accommodation involves the renunciation of protest or aggression against undesirable conditions of life and the organization of the character so that protest does not appear, but acceptance does. It may come to pass in the end that the unwelcome force is idealized, that one identifies with it and takes it into the personality" (250, 255). It is this insidious process that Angelou's southern contemporary powerfully describes in the following interview.

"TECH 'ER OFF, CHARLIE," IN TOM E. TERRILL AND JERROLD HIRSCH, EDS., *SUCH AS US: SOUTHERN VOICES OF THE THIRTIES* (Chapel Hill: University of North Carolina Press, 1978)

Johnston County, North Carolina, 1939

"Son, . . . a catfish is a lot like a nigger.
As long as he is in his mudhole he is all right,
but when he gits out he is in for a passel o' trouble."

"Lawd have mercy, you done axed me a question whut's gonna take quite a spell to answer. But if you is got de gumption to put up wid de way I tell it, I'll do de bes' I can."

Uncle Charlie Holcomb rammed his worn hands under the bib of his faded blue overalls. The chill of evening and the smell of fresh-turned earth crept in through the open doorway of his two-room cabin. The wide pine floorboards were scrubbed the color of bleached bone, and a bright fire crackled in the whitewashed fireplace. Uncle Charlie sat in a corner where he could 'tend the cornpone that baked in the coals. A pensive frown creased his forehead as he hitched his cane-bottomed chair closer [to] the fire.

"We has always been tenement farmers and my pappy before me was a tenement farmer. Used to be, when I was a young man, I thought I could manage my business better and dat I was gonna be able to own a place o' my own someday, but dey was always sumpthin' come along and knocked de props from under my plans. My 'baccer [tobacco] was either et up by de worms, or it was de rust or de blight, or pore prices—always sumpthin' to keep me from makin' dat little pot I planned on. And den time de lan'lord had took his share and de cost o' de fertilizer and de 'vancements he had made, dey wan't but jist enought to carry on till de nex' crop.

"But Lawdie Lawd, dat was back when I was a high-minded young nigger and was full of git-up-and-git. Dey wan't nothin' in de world dat I didn't think I could do, and I didn't have no patience wid niggers what didn't look for nothin' but sundown and payday.

"I 'members good as yestiddy 'bout de place whar I was borned. It was a little pine-board shack 'bout like dis one, down in Sampson County, and it was set on de top of a red clay hill 'bout a quarter of a mile from de big road. De yard was swep' clean and hard as dis floor, and us chillun used to play dere from sunup till sundown wid de houn' dogs and whatever we could fine ter fool wid. Law me! We didn't hab no fancy toys or nothin' like de chillun does now, but we got along. We drawed lines on de groun' and played hippity-hop and games like dat. Shucks, we didn't need no toys. Dey was eight of us kids and dey was enough fuss and racket goin' on among us to keep from gettin' lonesome.

"My pappy shore was a powerful man, and he believed in hard work. He riz at four o'clock every mornin' and rousted us chillun out as soon as he got a fire goin'. My mammy would hab on a pot o' grits and a slab o' salt pork and it shore sot good on our little bellies. Our land was mighty pore and durin' de growin' season we'd be in de fiel' by sunup. We always slep' a little atter dinner, den we'd go back and work till sundown. Dat is, de ones dat was big 'nough to work would, and de rest would stay at home and play, or maybe chunk de fire under mammy's washpot.

"My gran'pappy lived wid us too, but he wasn't able to do much work. He had de miseries in his back and walked wid a stick. But he was right handy 'bout things like sloppin' de hogs and feedin' de chickens. I was his pet chile too, and he holp me out a lot in de little things a chile has to learn growin' up. I was a frail chile and wan't able to work in de fields like most chillun. And gran'pappy looked out for me. When dey was wormin' and toppin' to be done, he would take me to dig bait for him, and den we would go to de crick and ketch a mess o' catfish. He used to do a heap o' thinkin' while we was sottin' dar fishin'. I 'member once he caught a big, fat catfish and jist played wid him for a long time. He pointed to de fish and tol' me to watch him. Den he lifted de fish outen de water and dat fish kicked and thrashed sumpthin' turrible. Den he lowered de line and let de fish back in de water. When he did dat de fish jist swum around as easy as you please. Den gran'pappy pulled de fish out on de bank and we watched him thrash around till he died. When de fish was dead gran'pappy turned to me. 'Son,' he said, 'a catfish is a lot like a nigger. As long as he is in his mudhole he is all right, but when he gits out he is in for a passel o' trouble. You 'member dat, and you won't have no trouble wid folks when you grows up.' But I was jist a kid den, and I couldn't make much out of it. I let dat plumb slip my mind, and later on it shore caused me a heap o' grief.

"Gran'pappy knowed a lot 'bout 'baccer, and de season for curin' come aroun' he would be de one to take care o' de firin' o' de 'baccer barn. We always did have a grand time durin' de curin', as we had ter stay wid de fire all de time 'til de 'baccer was done. Most o' de time some o' de neighbors would come over and bring a fiddle or a guitar and we would sing and dance and have de biggest kind o' time.

"I know how excited we all used to git when we started hangin' de 'baccer in de barn and gran'pappy would start layin' de wood for de fire. First he would put down some fat pine. Den he would lay some dry sticks on top o' dat, and last o' all he would put on some good sound hickory and white-oak sticks. It was always a great honor to light dat fire, and 'cause I was gran'pappy's pet he always let me do it. He would han' me a match and say, 'Tech 'er off, Charlie!'

"I was de las' chile to grow up and by dat time my mammy and pappy was gittin' pretty old. All de rest had either married or gone off to de public works, and I was de onliest one left to keep de ol' farm goin'. I never had been to school none to speak of, but I could read and write my name. All de time I kep' a-frettin' and a-hankerin' to git on a bigger farm and try to make sumpthin' outen myself. When de ol' folks died I lef' de place and moved over here to Johnston County and took a job on de public works. I saved me up a little money and married Dillie, and we took up dis place right whar we is now. Dat was over thirty year ago.

"Dis place was a lot bigger den dan it is now, but it don't take as much land for me now as when I was raisin' a family. I was full o' life den as a young bull, and meant to work hard and save my money and maybe buy de place later on. But like I done tol' you, dere was always sumpthin' dat come up to take all I had made. Back den dey wan't nothin' dat could disencourage me, and I kep' on a-tryin', and it wan't till my Willie was killed dat I lost de spirit.

"One time after I had sold all my 'baccer and de lan'lord took his share and de fertilizer money and de 'vancements out, it looked to me like I was gonna have a little left for myself. Den de warehouse man called me back and tol' me he had figgered wrong and dat I owed some more warehouse charges. I knowed it wa'n't right, and it made me so mad I jist hit him in de face as hard as I could. Den I kinda went crazy and might nigh beat him to death. I got twelve months on de roads for dat, and all de time I was away from home Dillie and de chillun had to try to make another crop, but 'course day couldn't do so good by deyselves and Mr. Crawford, dat's de lan'lord, had to carry 'em over. Hit took me three years to git him paid back.

"By dat time I knowed it wan't no use for me to try to ever make anything but jist a livin'. I was 'termined my oldest chile was gonna hab a chance in dis world, and I sent him all de way through high school. Willie was a mighty good boy and worked hard when he was at home.

"After he got outta high school he tol' me dat a man wid jist a high school eddycation couldn't git nowhere and dat he wanted to go to college. Me and Dillie talked it ober and we didn't see how we was a-gonna do it, but we let him go to de A & T College [the Agricultural and Technical College of North Carolina, now the North Carolina Agricultural and Technical State University, Greensboro, N.C.]. Will worked mighty hard and made good grades and worked out most o' his way. In de summer he would come home and he'p wid de 'baccer and we made some might good crops. Willie would take de 'baccer to market and go over de account, and he was pretty sharp and always come home wid money in his pocket.

"De last year Willie was in school he started gittin' fretful and sayin' dere wan't no future for a nigger in de 'baccer business, and dat he didn't want to come back to de farm. Dat hurt me, 'cause I had counted on Willie helpin' me, but I wanted him to do what he thought was best.

"When he graduated he was one o' de brightest boys in de class, but dat was when de trouble started. Willie knowed he had a good eddycation and didn't want to waste his time on no small job. But he couldn't find nothin' to do, and he finally come home and started settin' around and drinkin' and gittin' mean. I didn't know what was de matter wid him, and tried to reason wid him, but he wouldn' talk no sense wid me.

"Dat fall he took a load o' 'baccer to de warehouse, and when he come back he was all mad and sullen and I knowed he had been drinkin' again. All dat night he drunk and cussed sumpthin' turrible, and de nex' mornin' his eyes was all bloodshot and mean-lookin', and he had me scared. He said he was gonna take another load o' baccer to de warehouse, and I didn't want him to go, but he went anyway.

" 'Long 'bout dinnertime one o' de neighbors come a-runnin' wid his eyes bulgin' clean out on his cheeks. He said dere had been a fight at de warehouse and dat Willie had been hurt.

"I got on my ol' grey mule and rode into town as fast as I could. When I got to de warehouse I seen a bunch o' men standin' around and den I seen my Willie layin' on de ground and a great puddle o' blood around his head. I knowed he was dead de minute I seed him. For a while I didn't know what to do. I looked around at de crowd and dey wan't a friendly face nowhar. Right den I knowed dey wan't no use to ax for no he'p and dat I was jist a pore nigger in trouble. I picked my Willie up in my arms and saw his head was all bashed in. Dey was tears runnin' down my cheeks and droppin' on his face and I couldn't he'p it. I found de wagon he had driv' inter town and laid him in dat. Den I tied my ol' mule on behind and driv' home. I never did ax nobody 'bout what happened to de 'baccer he took in.

"When I got home I washed Willie's head and dressed him in his best suit. Den I went out to let Dillie hab her cry. We buried him at de foot o' dat big pine at de left o' de well, and made some grass to grow on de grave. Dat's de mound you was lookin' at as you come up to de house.

"For a long time atter dat I couldn't seem to git goin', and dey was a big chunk in de botton o' my stummick dat jist wouldn't go away. I would go out at night and set under de pine by Willie's grave, and listen to de win' swishin' in de needles, and I'd do a lot o' thinkin'.

"I knowed Willie had got killed 'cause he'd been in a argiment wid somebody at de warehouse. Den I got to thinkin' 'bout what gran'pappy said 'bout de catfish, and I knowed dat was de trouble wid Willie. He had stepped outen his place when he got dat eddycation. If I'd kept him here on de farm he woulda been all right. Niggers has got to l'arn dat dey ain't like white folks, and never will be, and no amount o' eddycation can make 'em be, and dat when dey gits outen dere place dere is gonna be trouble.

"Lots o' times dere is young bucks dat gits fretful wid de way things is, and wants to cut loose and change, and when dey comes talkin' around me I jist takes 'em out and shows 'em Willie's grave. I been turrible hurt 'bout losin' my Willie, but it has give me a peace o' mind dat I couldn't a-got nowhar else. My other chillun has all moved off and has famblies o' dere own and dey don't hab much, but dey is happy.

"White man didn't Jim Crow de nigger—it was God Jim Crowed 'im, back yonder when Ham laughed at pore ol' Noah for gettin' drunk. Niggers is built for service, like a mule, and dey needn't 'spect nothin' else. Dey has got to l'arn to leave de thinkin' and de plannin' to de white folks. Niggers ain't smart 'nough to do de things de white folks does. Dey couldn't 'vent no radio, nor a meter for measurin' how many feet o' 'lectricity a man uses, nor a autymobile, or none o' de gadgets we has nowdays. Dat's for de white folks to do. A nigger's place is in de field and de road and de tunnel and de woods, wid a pick or shovel or ax or hoe or plow. God made a nigger like a mule to be close to nature and git his livin' by de sweat o' his brow like de Good Book says. And when a nigger is workin' and feelin' de strength o' his muscles and de good hot sun in his face he is happy. Long as he has plenty o' cornpone and pot likker to wash it down wid, he don't need nothin' else.

"I don't work much more like I used to. De chillun drap by now and den and he'p me wid de crops. I don't pay much 'tention to whether de prices for 'baccer is good or bad, 'cause I knows I always has 'nough to git by on. De lan'lord has been mighty good to me, and don't worry me in de least no more. I has my hog meat and plenty o' meal and collards in de summer, and Dillie always cans a little sumpthin' for de winter. Maybe I'se gittin' too ol' to care any more, but I knows de white folks takes pretty good care o' dere niggers, and I don't never worry 'bout whether my home is gonna be took by a mortgage or not. I has plenty to eat, 'cause my cravin's ain't very fancy, and I has plenty o' time to let my mind wander.

"Sometimes I git to dozin' and noddin' by de fire, and thinks back 'bout de time when I was a chile on my pappy's place. We didn't have nothin' much to wear, or much to eat, but we was happy. And I 'member how my gran'pappy used to pet me and take me fishin' wid him. Seems like when a feller thinks back he only 'members de good parts. De barn is always full o' yeller 'baccer, ready to be fired, and de kids all runnin' around whoppin' and hollerin' and somebody a-pickin' a banjo, and de air full o' de scent o' fryin' side-meat and cornpone. I can almos' see gran'pappy down on his knees pullin' out a big fat splinter and handin' me a match and sayin', 'Tech 'er off, Charlie!' " (254–259)

Author unknown

STUDY QUESTIONS

1. How did slave owners ensure their physical and psychological dominance over their slaves?

2. What was the psychological legacy of slavery after Emancipation?

3. What economic, social, and cultural conditions contributed to the oppression of African Americans after slavery?

4. Why did African Americans become the primary targets of lynching?

5. Describe the profile of the typical participant in a lynching.

6. What effect did the threat of lynching have on African Americans?

7. What were some other techniques of social control designed to keep African Americans in the roles defined for them by whites?

8. What are the intentions of the racial etiquette? In other words, for whose benefit does the racial etiquette exist? Give some examples of the term.

9. Why was there little organized resistance to the oppression of African Americans until the 1960s?

TOPICS FOR WRITTEN OR ORAL EXPLORATION

1. According to your reading of *I Know Why the Caged Bird Sings*, what was the racial environment in Stamps, Arkansas? Were the social control techniques discussed here effective in Stamps? Explain.

2. Why did African Americans fail to achieve economic parity with whites after Emancipation? Use examples from "Tech 'Er Off, Charlie" and *I Know Why the Caged Bird Sings* to illustrate your answer.

3. Compare and contrast Momma's attitude toward whites with the views expressed by Charlie Holcomb in "Tech 'Er Off, Charlie."

4. Maya believes her grandmother comes out the winner in her encounter with the powhitetrash children at the store. Why does she think so? Do you agree? Explain.

5. What effect does the climate of racial prejudice have on Maya's psychological development? What is the significance for Maya of the episode with Mrs. Cullinan?

6. Charlie Holcomb appears resigned to his place in southern society. What factors have contributed to his abandoning his ambitions? Does Maya share his resignation? Why or why not?

7. Judging from the documents in this chapter and your reading of *I Know Why the Caged Bird Sings*, how did African American parents

prepare their children to live in an environment of racial prejudice? What do you think of their methods?

WORKS CITED

Angelou, Maya. *Gather Together in My Name*. New York: Random House, 1974.

————. *I Know Why the Caged Bird Sings*. 1970. Toronto: Bantam Books, 1971.

Boyd, R. H. *The Separate or "Jim Crow" Car Laws or Legislative Enactments of Fourteen Southern States*. Nashville: National Baptist Publishing Board, 1909.

Dollard, John. *Caste and Class in a Southern Town*. New York: Oxford University Press, 1938.

Goldfield, David R. *Black, White, and Southern: Race Relations and Southern Culture 1940 to the Present*. Baton Rouge: Louisiana State University Press, 1990.

Karon, Bertram P. *The Negro Personality: A Rigorous Investigation of the Effects of Culture*. New York: Springer, 1958.

Kennedy, Stetson. *Jim Crow Guide to the U.S.A.: The Laws, Customs and Etiquette Governing the Conduct of Nonwhites and Other Minorities as Second-Class Citizens*. Westport, Conn.: Greenwood Press, 1959.

Lynchings and What They Mean: General Findings of the Southern Commission on the Study of Lynching. Atlanta: The Commission, 1931.

Tolnay, Stewart E., and E. M. Beck. *A Festival of Violence: An Analysis of Southern Lynchings, 1882–1930*. Urbana and Chicago: University of Illinois Press, 1995.

SUGGESTED READINGS

See the full text of works excerpted in this chapter.

For more on the social practices of segregation, see:

Johnson, Claudia D. "Historical Context: The Civil Rights Movement." In *Understanding "To Kill a Mockingbird."* Westport, Conn.: Greenwood Press, 1994.

Woodward, C. Vann. *The Strange Career of Jim Crow*. New York: Oxford University Press, 1974.

For more information on lynching, see:

Ames, Jessie Daniel. *The Changing Character of Lynching: Review of Lynching, 1931–1941, with a Discussion of Recent Developments in This Field*. Atlanta: Commission on Interracial Cooperation, 1942.

Raper, Arthur. *The Tragedy of Lynching*. Chapel Hill: University of North Carolina Press, 1933.

The following works provide further information on the racial etiquette:

Angelou, Maya. *Creativity* with Bill Moyers. Corporation for Entertainment and Learning, Inc. WNET Thirteen. New York, 1982.

Doyle, Bertram Wilbur. *The Etiquette of Race Relations in the South: A Study in Social Control*. 1937. New York: Schocken Books, 1971.

Moton, Robert Russa. *What the Negro Thinks*. Garden City, N.Y.: Doubleday, Doran, 1929.

These Are Our Lives. Chapel Hill: University of North Carolina Press, 1939.

A final work of historical interest:

Alexander, Charles C. *The Ku Klux Klan in the Southwest*. Lexington: University of Kentucky Press, 1965.

3

Segregated Schools: An Institutional Method of Social Control

Segregation had a profound impact on the quality of the education available to African Americans in the South. In addition to the methods discussed in the previous chapter, legal mandates for separate, and by extension, unequal schools were another means of exercising control over the lives of African Americans by limiting the opportunities available to them to improve their social status and employment options. In *White and Negro Schools in the South*, Pierce et al. note, "It was but natural that in a region which viewed the Negro as being an inferior person that separate school systems would develop" (17). The concept of separate schools was upheld in the now famous court case *Plessy vs. Ferguson* (1896), which challenged a Louisiana statute requiring separate but equal accommodations on trains for blacks and whites (see the discussion in Chapter 2). The plaintiff, Homer Adolph Plessy, claimed that the Louisiana statute violated the Thirteenth and Fourteenth Amendments to the U.S. Constitution. In upholding the constitutionality of the law, the court wrote:

> The object of the [Fourteenth] amendment was undoubtedly to enforce the absolute equality of the two races before the law, but, in the nature of things, it could not have been intended to abolish distinctions based upon color, or to enforce social, as distinguished

from political, equality, or a commingling of the two races upon terms unsatisfactory to either. Laws permitting, and even requiring, their separation, in places where they are liable to be brought into contact, do not necessarily imply the inferiority of either race to the other, and have been generally, if not universally, recognized as within the competency of the state legislatures in the exercise of their police power. *The most common instance of this is connected with the establishment of separate schools for white and colored children, which have been held to be a valid exercise of the legislative power even by courts of states where the political rights of the colored race have been longest and most earnestly enforced* [emphasis added]. (1140)

Pierce et al. write that as a result of the ruling in *Plessy vs. Ferguson*, "the separate but equal doctrine was accepted as a principle throughout the region, apparently by both races, by the beginning of the twentieth century" (17). A direct challenge to the principle of segregation in the public schools did not succeed until 1954, when the Supreme Court, in *Brown vs. Board of Education of Topeka, Kansas*, said: "We conclude that in the field of public education the doctrine of 'separate but equal' has no place. Separate educational facilities are inherently unequal" (quoted in Pierce et al., 22).

Indeed, during the first half of the twentieth century, conditions in the schools attended by blacks were vastly inferior to those found in schools attended by white students. Not only were the facilities at black schools inadequate, but the quality of teaching was often second-rate. Standards for African American teachers were dismally low. Angelou writes of her pride before her eighth-grade graduation ceremony, exulting in the fact that many of the teachers in African American schools in Arkansas had only attended school through the eighth grade. In "Public Education: The Battle and Its Aftermath," Harry A. Johnson observes that in the early years of the twentieth century "47,426 Negro teachers were certified in fifteen southern states, but many had not been educated beyond the fifth grade. In 1930, more than one-third of southern Negro teachers possessed less than a high school training and fewer than 58 percent of these teachers had less than two years of college training" (23).

African American teachers were paid far less than their white counterparts, so there was little hope of attracting more qualified staff. In addition, the higher teacher-student ratios created difficult working conditions for African American teachers. Comparative data for white and black schools in seventeen states and the District of Columbia from the *Statistical Summary of Education, 1939–40* show that an average of 29.2 white students were enrolled per member of instructional staff (principals, supervisors, and teachers); for African American students the figure was much higher: 37.7. In Arkansas the average was 33.7 for white students and 44.0 for black students in the same period.

A final factor contributing to the poor education received by African American children was the need to work during harvest time. Families were often obliged to keep children out of school for lengthy periods so that they could help in the fields, a circumstance that helps to account for the poor attendance records of many African American students.

But despite the overall bleak picture, some efforts at reforms were made. Self-studies undertaken by the states themselves, as well as national surveys of education like the one cited above, acknowledged the inequalities and included recommendations for change. In addition, several northern foundations provided funds for new schools, equipment, teacher training, and curricular reform. The Lafayette County Training School, which Angelou attended, was a direct result of this type of intervention.

The documents in this chapter provide further insight into conditions in African American schools and the attempts made to improve them. The first section deals with general conditions in African American schools in the South before World War II, particularly during the 1930s and early 1940s, while the second section provides extensive documentation of conditions prevalent in Arkansas in the 1920s. The documents in the third section explore the county training school concept. The chapter concludes with consideration of the attitudes of African Americans toward education as documented in a study published in 1941.

CONDITIONS IN AFRICAN AMERICAN SCHOOLS IN THE SOUTH BEFORE WORLD WAR II

The two documents in this section serve as a general introduction to the conditions prevalent in schools attended by African Americans in the South before World War II, when Angelou was a child in Arkansas. Ina Corinne Brown's national survey of education gives general statistics comparing white schools and black schools in terms of funding, length of school year, and teacher salaries. In addition, the document describes typical school facilities for African Americans and notes their lack of access to cultural institutions such as museums and public libraries that would enhance community educational opportunities.

Excerpts from Charles Johnson's book about youth growing up in the South also include statistics that show how inadequately funded schools attended by blacks were compared to those attended by whites. Johnson provides a valuable account of a typical African American school, describing the inside and outside of the facility at Dine Hollow, the attitude of the teacher, and the day's lessons for the four grades taught by her in one classroom. His work offers direct insight into the poor educational experience available to most African American students. Like Brown, Johnson also discusses teacher salaries and teacher qualifications.

The information presented in these two documents is consistent with the picture Angelou draws of the contrast between her school and the local school for white students (*I Know Why the Caged Bird Sings*, 143). One can conclude that African Americans generally lacked access to high-quality education in the South's segregated schools.

INA CORINNE BROWN, *NATIONAL SURVEY OF THE HIGHER EDUCATION OF NEGROES: SOCIO-ECONOMIC APPROACH TO EDUCATIONAL PROBLEMS*
(Washington, D.C.: Federal Security Agency, U.S. Office of Education, Misc. No. 6, Vol. 1., GPO, 1942)

In addition to the economic and occupational restrictions placed upon him, the Negro finds himself seriously handicapped in his effort to secure an education. . . . [T]he Negro child receives, on the average, a little more than a third of the school funds allotted the white child; his school term is often from 1 to 3 months shorter than the term for white children; and his teachers are paid lower salaries than white teachers of comparable training. While the number of high schools for Negroes has increased very rapidly in recent decades there are still many areas in which no high-school facilities are available.

In a study of two typical black belt counties Arthur Raper found that in 80 or more percent of the rural Negro schools the pupils had no desks but used church pews or benches which necessitated their holding books and writing materials in their laps. Throughout the South there are thousands of 1-room schools for Negroes. Other thousands of schools are held in churches, lodge halls, or abandoned shacks. Transportation to consolidated schools is generally lacking for Negro children, and school equipment is often wholly inadequate or nonexistent.

The lack of adequate educational facilities has serious social and economic consequences. The short term of the rural school results in retardation and an excessive piling up of pupils in the lower grades. Of the population on relief in the eastern cotton area in October 1935, 1 in 4 white heads of households, and only 1 in 25 of the Negro heads of households had advanced beyond the seventh grade in school.

The Negro's minority group position affects not only his formal educational opportunity but also his civic opportunity and his access to cultural facilities. In the region in which the majority of Negroes live they are generally excluded from libraries, museums, and art galleries. Only rarely are separate services provided, and these are usually of an inferior sort. According to Louis R. Wilson, in 1926 there were 45 public libraries for Negroes in 12 of the Southern States. In 1935 the number had increased to 75. More than 80 percent of the Negro population were outside library service districts and of the 491 counties listed as service districts only 75 actually provided service to Negroes.

In theaters, concert halls, and public auditoriums of southern towns the Negro is either excluded or permitted to occupy only some special section which he must usually reach through a side or back entrance. Rural communities seldom have even this provision for Negroes. Parks, gymnasiums, and swimming pools are seldom available to Negroes in the areas in which they are most needed. In rural counties in which the church or the school might become the center of community life, the minister or the teacher rarely has the training or equipment necessary for leadership. The striking photographs made by Arthur Raper of the schoolhouses for Negroes in certain rural areas suggest that in many places the school building would be the last place to which one would willingly go for any purpose. Raper closes his chapter on recreational facilities with the pointed remark that "The rural family does not need more places to go so much as better places to go, particularly better schools and churches, and above all more interesting things to stay at home with." (42–43)

CHARLES S. JOHNSON, *GROWING UP IN THE BLACK BELT: NEGRO YOUTH IN THE RURAL SOUTH*
(Washington, D.C.: American Council on Education, 1941)

What about the schools for southern rural youth? How far does the public school compensate for the disadvantages of poor homes and neighborhoods, economic distress, and lack of opportunity for personality development? As we shall see, the public schools open to southern rural Negroes can contribute very little to the elevation of these youth. . . .

Financing

Although the rate of taxation is relatively high in the southern states, there is not enough tax revenue to maintain governmental services comparable to those in other states. Nowhere is this inadequacy more evident than in the funds appropriated for rural Negro schools. To be sure, a school which carries out a progressive program of education is costly, and one should not expect to find excellent school systems in impoverished states. The point here, however, is that in the South the school funds, which are usually insufficient to support one good school system, are unequally divided. Only a small amount of the available tax revenue is expended on Negro education.

It is, of course, regrettable that, whereas the average annual expenditure for schooling (current expense, interest, and capital outlay) per pupil in average daily attendance in 1937–38 was $99.70 in the United States as a whole, in the South where separate schools for Negroes and whites are maintained it was $60.61 in the 17 states and the District of Columbia. It is more unfortunate that the per capita expenditure for Negro youth in average daily attendance is only $23.00 in the 12 southern states where information is available. . . .

Throughout the South the county superintendents usually find that tax revenues are too meager to support even a single efficient school system. Legal requirements and tradition have complicated this problem by the biracial educational system. Inevitably the outcome is that Negro schools are allotted only a small share of funds which, even on an equal division, would hardly suffice. It is frequently explained, by way of justification, that this inequality is necessary because the Negro is too impoverished to pay school taxes. The fact remains, however, that the burden of indirect taxation falls as heavily upon the Negro as upon anyone else.

Quality of Instruction

The homes of rural Negro youth are, with few exceptions, dismally inadequate. Their schools, which have the support of the state, are scarcely better. Unattractive schools and a lack of supplies for class work do little to inspire pupils with aesthetic feelings or to induce teachers to put forth their best efforts. Teachers on a bare subsistence income, and often with a minimum of preparation, are hardly qualified to foster the development of wholesome, well-adjusted personalities in their pupils.

A typical rural Negro school is at Dine Hollow. It is in a dilapidated building, once whitewashed, standing in a rocky field unfit for cultivation. Dust-dovered weeds spread a carpet all around, except for an uneven, bare area on one side which looks like a ball field. Behind the school is a small building with a broken, sagging door. As we approach, a nervous, middle-aged woman comes to the door of the school. She greets us in a discouraged voice marred by a speech impediment. Escorted inside, we observe that the broken benches are crowded to three times their normal capacity. Only a few battered books are in sight, and we look in vain for maps or charts. We learn that four grades are assembled here. The weary teacher agrees to permit us to remain while she proceeds with the instruction. She goes to the blackboard and writes an assignment for the first two grades to do while she conducts spelling and word drills for the third and the fourth grades. This is the assignment:

> Write your name ten times.
> Draw an dog, an cat, an rat, an boot.
> Draw an tree, an house, an cow, an goat.
> Draw an book, an apple, an tomatoe.

While the children are complying with these instructions, the older ones are reciting:

Teacher: What is a contraction?

Pupil: A word with a letter left out.

Teacher: What word would rhyme with "hung"?

Pupil: Rung.

Teacher: Give me a little word that we make longer by adding "ing."

Pupil: Read.

Teacher: How would you write "G-o-d"?

Pupil: Capital "G."

Teacher: How can you pluralize the word "jelly"?

Pupil: Change "y" to "i."

Teacher: You add "er" to what word to make it longer?

Pupil: Old.

Teacher: Now we have the word "win." To add "ing" what do you do?

Pupil: Double the last letter in the word.

Next, the arithmetic class is called up for recitation. These fourth-graders have to multiply and to check their products. One boy demonstrates the method of checking. He multiplies 32 by 4 and obtains 128; he then writes 32 down four times and adds to check the answer. To be doubly sure of their answers the children all count on their fingers in addition. We inspect a child's paper and read as follows:

a. 158	158	b. 204	204
4	158	6	204
632	158	1,224	204
	158		204
	632		204
			204
			1,224

Another class comes forward to recite on the day's reading lesson. Haltingly a boy retells the story which the group had been assigned to read:

> Fred was little boy. He went to the city to work for a man. The man told him if he worked he would pay him. Fred worked three years. The man paid him only three pennies. Fred said . . . Fred said . . . The man paid him only three pennies. Fred said . . .

The poor boy could get no further; he simply could not recall what Fred had said. Obviously the story had been studied in rote fashion, as no amount of questioning by the teacher served to refresh this pupil's memory.

In the English class there is a "review" on the kinds of verbs. "How many kinds of verbs are there?" the teacher inquires. A volunteer opens the lessons by replying, "Adverbs . . ." but is interrupted by the teacher. "There are two kinds of verbs, aren't there?" she says. "Yes," the class agrees. "They are transitive and intransitive, aren't they?" And again the class agrees with her. So the lesson proceeds with the teacher answering as well as asking the questions and the class voicing their agreement.

At another school in the county the teacher came forward with her face wrapped up in a white cloth. "I am suffering from neuralgia," she explains. "We have no substitute teachers here, and when one of us gets sick we just have to keep right on. I'll just keep the children busy today. I don't feel like teaching.'' So she requests the fourth-graders to write all they know about fish—where they live, how they are caught, and how they are canned. Second-graders have two assignments: first, they must draw three boots, two eyes, and a stone; then they are to use *one, two, three, girl, boy, baby* in sentences. At the board the teacher draws in crude fashion these objects which the first-grade children are to identify: an apple, a pear, an eye, an ear, a spider's web, and an ice cream cone.

No doubt, the very low salaries paid to Negro teachers in the rural districts are one cause for instruction such as is illustrated by these typical examples. Few well-trained persons would be attracted to teaching for the amounts paid, and few teachers could spare money to pay for necessary in-service training. Another reason for such low quality instruction is that appointments are often made on the basis of political influence and personal manipulation. Often county superintendents are not particularly interested in the Negro schools within their jurisdiction, and they make appointments in a most casual manner. Personal acquaintance with the superintendent, a reputation for efficiency in domestic or personal service, and recommendations from influential white citizens often carry more weight than training and experience.

The results of such a lack of concern for the professional qualifications of applicants for teaching positions in rural Negro schools are plainly evident. In 1931 Horace Mann Bond gave the Stanford Achievement Test to 306 Negro teachers enrolled in summer school who had been teaching during 1930–31 in the public schools of six Alabama counties. He reported that these teachers made an average score below the national norm set for ninth-grade school children. Elizabeth Moore depicted the situation in more dramatic language when we interviewed her:

> The teachers in Boyle [Mississippi] were worse than they are in Alabama. You won't believe this, but it is the honest-to-God's truth. We had one teacher who didn't know her multiplication tables. She didn't mind telling us that she didn't know. She'd say to us, when we'd ask her what a certain number multiplied by a certain number was, "Oh, go away, child, I am tired and can't be bothered with you. If I tried to remember all that study and stuff I'd go crazy." We soon found that she didn't know a lot of things so we always thought of hard things to ask her so she would be embarrassed 'cause she didn't know them. I told mamma about this when I got home and she decided to move to Bolivar. Here the schools are better, the terms longer, and the teachers are better. We have the best school in the county. If I hadn't been thrown back in those other schools I would have finished before I was 18.

As Elizabeth has said, the school term in many rural districts is very short. Four Alabama counties had an average term of less than five months, and the average term in Negro schools throughout the state was about seven months in 1936–37. The teachers are, themselves, the products of an inadequate system, and merely help to perpetuate its unfortunate results. (102–7)

THE EDUCATION OF AFRICAN AMERICANS
IN ARKANSAS

In 1923 the federal government published an in-depth analysis of the state of public education in Arkansas, where Angelou attended school. One section of the report, entitled "Public Schools for Negroes," is reprinted here. The topics covered include population, agriculture, public school statistics, enrollment and attendance, distribution of pupils through the grades, illiteracy, teachers, test scores, supervision, foundation support, and county training schools. The document concludes with a summary and some recommendations for change.

Many of the problems characteristic of African American schools in the South as a whole were found in the Arkansas schools as well. Cost of instruction per child enrolled for African Americans in Arkansas was approximately one-third the sum spent on white students; 63.1 black students were enrolled per teacher versus 39.9 white students per teacher. Teachers were poorly prepared and underpaid, receiving about one-half the salary earned by white teachers; attendance was poor, the rate of illiteracy was high, and many students were in lower grades than would be expected for their age group.

Despite these gross inequities, the report does not advocate desegregation. However, it expresses enthusiastic support for vocational training for African American students, such as agriculture and home economics (see the discussion under "The Jeanes Fund," for example). In addition, the discussion of county training schools is of special interest, as Angelou attended the Lafayette County Training School.

U.S. DEPARTMENT OF THE INTERIOR, BUREAU OF EDUCATION,
"THE PUBLIC SCHOOL SYSTEM OF ARKANSAS: REPORT OF A
SURVEY MADE UNDER THE DIRECTION OF THE UNITED
STATES COMMISSIONER OF EDUCATION AT THE REQUEST OF
THE ARKANSAS STATE EDUCATIONAL COMMISSION. PART I."
(*Bulletin*. 1923, 10 [Washington, D.C.: GPO, 1923])

Public Schools for Negroes

The negro population of Arkansas is 472,220, according to the 1920 census, and forms 27 per cent of the total. The negroes are located chiefly in the counties on or near the Mississippi River and in the southern part of the State. The negro population in the northern and western parts of the State is very small. Most of the northern counties, and especially those in the northwestern part of the State, have very few negroes. Of the 75 counties in the State, 37 have a negro population constituting less than 12.5 per cent of the total population of those counties. There are 26 counties in which the negro population of school age is less than 1,000, and in 19 of these the school population is less than 500.

The negroes form a very large and important group of people. From an agricultural standpoint the importance of the negro can hardly be overstated. The census of 1920 reported 15,373 negro farm owners, or 14.9 per cent of the total number, 102,647. Of the 121,221 farm tenants reported, 56,814 are negroes, or 46.8 per cent. In 1920 there were 72,187 negro farmers (tenants and owners) reported, and these farmers constitute 31.2 per cent of all persons engaged in agriculture in Arkansas. Between 1910 and 1920 the number of farms operated by negroes increased 8,689, or 13.6 per cent. As owners and tenants they farm 2,624,726 acres.

From the standpoint of public health alone, however, the white people of Arkansas must be concerned about the welfare of the negroes. There is no such thing as protecting the welfare of a part of the people. It is possible to safeguard the health of all, or to protect the health of none. A close student of southern conditions has described the situation in one sentence by saying "A germ is color blind." It is a well-known fact that widespread ignorance and illiteracy are generally productive of insanitary conditions, and hence of diseases. The health of the white people in Arkansas can not be considered as independent and separate from the health of the negroes.

Eighty-nine per cent of the negro population is located in 31 counties, and half of this 89 per cent is concentrated in 11 counties. In the other 44 counties the negro population is too small to constitute any large burden, so far as the expense of education is concerned. It is true, how-

ever, that in some counties the problem of providing schools for the
negroes is made more difficult by the fact that the numbers are small and
sometimes scattered over a relatively large area.

The statement is sometimes made that in Arkansas the cost of maintaining public schools is relatively greater because separate schools must
be provided for the negroes. The presence of the negro does complicate
the educational situation to the extent that it makes necessary the maintenance of two school systems. But it should be borne in mind that even
if the entire population of the State were white it would be necessary to
provide far more teachers and schoolhouses than are now provided for
the white population, with a resultant increase in cost to the State.

Public-School Statistics

	White	Negro
Population of school age, 1920	482,336	192,665
Enrollment, 1920	367,198	131,084
Cost of instruction, 1920	$6,281,768	$735,222
Cost of Instruction per child enrolled	$17.06	$5.61
Number of teachers, 1920	9,693	2,076
Pupils enrolled per teacher	39.9	63.1
Average attendance, 1920	262,289	86,755
Per cent of enrolled attending	71.4	66.2
Per cent of school population attending	54.4	45.0

The table shows that the annual cost of instruction, based on enrollment, is $17.06 for the white pupils and $5.61 for the colored. The figures are taken from the official records of the State department of public
instruction. Even if it be assumed that the negro schools are efficient, no
great return can be reasonably expected on an annual expenditure of
$5.61 per pupil enrolled. It must be borne in mind, too, that a large
number of negro children who should be attending school are not even
enrolled.

The negro schools should be consolidated so far as possible. If larger
negro schools were built, the number of negro schools could be reduced
and most of the one-teacher and two-teacher schools eliminated. This
would mean increased school efficiency as in the case of the white
schools. While free transportation would be necessary for some white
pupils, it would not be necessary for the negroes on account of the large
negro population in these 11 counties, and the same thing may be said
with regard to a number of other counties.

In some instances there is very marked disparity between the per capita expenditures for white pupils and for colored. In Helena, for example, the figures are $68.12 and $12.60; in Magnolia, $23.57 and $3.21; in Wynne, $24.29 and $6.02; and in Monticello, $27.44 and $4.85. It may be said in behalf of Helena that, while the disparity between the amounts is great, the per capita expenditures for negro pupils is fairly reasonable in amount. But this can not be said of Wynne, Magnolia, and Monticello, and a number of other towns in the list.

In cities the white pupils are all living within a small area, and there is no reason why there should be a large per capita expenditure as a result of having a small number of pupils per teacher, except in the case of high-school classes.

Of the larger cities, Fort Smith and Hot Springs deserve to be commended for their fair treatment of the negro school children. Of the smaller cities, Fardyce has one of the most efficient negro schools in the State, and the per capita amounts spent on white and colored pupils show a decided disposition to give the negroes fair consideration. There is less excuse for disparity between per capita expenditures in towns than in rural districts, as rural conditions make the school problem more difficult.

Enrollment and Attendance

There are 61,581 negro children of school age who are not enrolled, and there are 44,329 who do not attend school regularly. The total number of those not enrolled and not attending is 105,910. The fact that the average attendance in negro schools is actually less than half of the negro population of a school age is a sad commentary on the school situation in Arkansas. Since 27 per cent of the State's population is colored this condition is one that challenges the statesmanship of Arkansas and calls for heroic measures.

Distribution of Pupils Through the Grades

An attempt was made to secure data concerning ages, and grades in which enrolled, of all colored pupils in Arkansas. Many teachers and principals neglected to supply this information, so that reports are available for only 22,588 pupils, approximately one-fourth of the average number reported as in attendance in 1920.

The large proportion of children in each grade who are too old for the grades in which they are enrolled is apparent.

Pupils of all ages from 8 years to 21 years of age, inclusive, are found in the sixth grade, a spread of 14 years; pupils 12 years of age are found in every grade from the first year of the elementary school to the fourth year of high school; other facts may be noted in the table.

Illiteracy in Arkansas

It is apparent that the negro schools did not accomplish much in the reduction of illiteracy in this age group. Between 1910 and 1920 the number of illiterate negroes 21 years of age and over must have been reduced by death, but this loss was practically offset by the number of illiterate negroes who reached the age of 21 during the same period. If the negro schools had been doing efficient work, and enrolling a reasonably large percentage of the school population, the difference between the number of adult negro male illiterates in 1921 and 1920 would certainly have been larger than 580. The fact that the percentage of adult negro male illiteracy was reduced only 3.4 per cent in 10 years must be alarming to any one who is concerned about progress in Arkansas. The negro schools are evidently exerting only a negligible influence on the problem of adult illiteracy in Arkansas.

Summary

Illiteracy in Arkansas is largely negro illiteracy, since the 79,254 illiterate negroes 10 years of age and over form 21.8 per cent of the negro population in that age group and 6.1 per cent of the State's population in that age group. This is a distressing amount of illiteracy. The fact that somewhat similar conditions exist in States like Georgia and Mississippi, where the negro population is larger than it is in Arkansas, does not improve conditions in this State. A degree of illiteracy shown by the figures given above means a shocking waste of human energy. The actual loss in money due to agricultural and industrial inefficiency can not be computed, but it must be an enormous sum.

The figures show that in the 10 years between 1910 and 1920 the progress made in elimination of negro illiteracy was not satisfactory.

This is not a matter of mystery. It is very easy to see how the present regrettable condition will perpetuate itself indefinitely unless the school facilities are improved. With a negro school population of 192,665, an enrollment of 131,084, and an average attendance of 86,755, or 45 per cent of the school population, it is very evident that a new crop of illiterates is coming on to replace those removed by death.

Teachers in Negro Schools

There are 2,076 negro public-school teachers in Arkansas. As the enrollment in negro schools is 131,084, there are 63.1 pupils enrolled per teacher. In the white schools there are 39.9 pupils enrolled per teacher. The number of negro teachers is obviously too small for the enrollment.

It is reasonable to suppose that as a rule the higher the grades of license a teacher holds the more efficient the teacher is. The grade of license is certainly a measure of the teacher's knowledge of subject matter. No teacher can hope to impart to others a knowledge that he himself does not have. The State and professional licenses are the highest issued. The number of negro teachers holding these is negligible. On the other hand, 63.6 per cent hold second and third grade licenses, the two grades representing the least scholarship.

The most significant figures are those showing that 38 per cent of the teachers in the larger places and 48 per cent of those in places of less than 200 population have had no high-school training. Even larger proportions have had no normal or college work, even in summer sessions. A discouragingly small number meet what should be regarded as the minimum requirements, namely, graduation from four-year high school plus two years of normal-school training for elementary teachers and graduation from four-year college, including professional courses, for high-school teachers. Of the teachers reporting only a small proportion are professionally prepared to teach. This is simply another way of saying that the negro schools of Arkansas are so inefficient that a considerable part of the $735,222 spent annually on the instruction of negro children is spent to little purpose, so far as educational results are concerned.

Nearly three-fourths (73.6 per cent) of the negro school children enrolled in the schools of Arkansas are in the first four grades. On the principle of "The greatest good to the greatest number," the pupils in the lower grades should have the best teachers available.

Educationally speaking, "the slaughter of the innocents" represented by the elimination of pupils between the first and second grades, the second and third, and so on, is due in large measure to inefficient teaching in the primary grades.

The figures also show the almost complete lack of grading or classification of the children. More than two-thirds of all the negro children in the schools are too old for the grades in which they are enrolled. In grades 4, 5, 6, and 7 this is true of four-fifths or more of the children.

The rapid elimination of pupils from school shows the futility of expecting the aims of public education to be accomplished so long as conditions remain as they are. In three or four short terms of two to five months each it is impossible to give the average child that amount of education and preparation for life which is essential to the maintenance of our democratic institutions. The present and future safety of the State demand adequate remedies for these conditions.

Most of the negro teachers in Arkansas began their teaching careers in the State, and have done all of their teaching there. Generally speaking, they are an experienced group; more than three-fourths have had more than three years' experience. At the same time it is to be noted that nearly one-half (46.1 per cent) had taught less than one year in their present positions at the time of report to the survey.

There are some marked discrepancies between the pay of white and colored teachers. In St. Francis County the pay of negro teachers in city schools is less than half that of white teachers. In Ouachita and Monroe Counties the negro teachers receive a monthly salary about one-half that given the white teachers. It must be remembered in this connection that the negro teachers are expected to teach larger numbers of pupils than the white teachers are. The inefficiency of the negro schools, however, is due to the ratio of teachers to pupils, as well as to underpaid teachers.

Scores in Spelling Test

A test in spelling was given to 1,304 pupils in grades 2 to 11, inclusive, in 40 negro schools, in 22 counties.

In all grades except 10 and 11 the words used were chosen from lists in which the standard of accuracy, as shown by tests of thousands of pupils, is 73. The pupils in grades 10 and 11 were given the words selected for the ninth grade. The results of this test are not conclusive for other subjects, but suggest low standards of achievement in the colored schools. The average score in the colored schools was 52.

State Supervision of Schools

Through the cooperation of the General Education Board, a rural school agent connected with the State department of public instruction, and working under the direction of the State superintendent of public instruction, gives his entire time to supervising the negro public schools of the State. The rural school agent is a white man of extended experience in school work, and he organizes and directs certain phases of the colored school work. The county training schools are under his supervision. He has charge of expending the funds given the State by the Slater Fund, the General Education Board, and the Rosenwald Fund. When the Jeanes Fund was being used in Arkansas, there were 21 county industrial supervisers. The rural school agent was employed so that the proper supervision and direction might be given the Jeanes industrial teachers. Since he began his work, however, the amount given the State by the Rosenwald Fund has been greatly increased, so that a large part of his time is now devoted to the supervision of schoolhouse construction. It is his duty to approve and submit applications for aid on new buildings and to see that the buildings are erected according to plan and are completed within eight months after application is approved. He makes the payments on the buildings and reports on partially complete and finished buildings as payments are made.

There is a colored man known as "Rosenwald Agent" who helps the rural school agent in this work. The Rosenwald Fund pays $1,200 of this agent's salary and the balance is paid by the Agricultural, Mechanical and Normal College. Due to this worker's efforts, a larger amount of money is secured for Rosenwald buildings as more schools are built. The rural school agent can not give all his time to this work and the help of the assistant is very valuable.

It is doubtful whether any school funds spent in Arkansas produce more real results than the Smith-Hughes money spent at colored schools.

The instruction is based on the project plan and is very effective. This work in Arkansas compares favorably, as to quality, with similar work in other States. The striking success scored in this work may be attributed to the following factors:

(1) Well-trained teachers who have the technical training needed for successful work.

(2) The teachers are employed for 12 months and are well paid, the salaries ranging from $1,200 to $1,800.

(3) The work is supervised by the teacher-trainer and the rural-school agent.

(4) Sufficient time is devoted to the work—half of each day.

(5) The work is related to the needs of the pupils and holds their interest.

(6) The project method of teaching is used, so that technical instruction and practical work go hand in hand.

The Jeanes Fund

In 1918–19 the sum of $2,836 was secured from the Jeanes Fund and $3,159 from the General Education Board, a total of $5,995. This money was used to pay part of the salary of industrial supervising teachers in 21 counties. These workers were employed for 11 months. They visited all the schools in the 21 counties, teaching handicrafts, such as basketry and shuck-mat making. They also taught plain sewing and gave cooking demonstrations in the homes of the pupils. After the school term they worked with the girls' clubs organized during the school term. The object of this "home-makers' club" work was the improvement of rural life. Demonstrations were given in cooking, canning, and preserving. No money ever spent in Arkansas produced more results. Such a large number of children were reached by these workers that the per capita cost was small indeed. The program was very practical and the activities introduced into the schools by these teachers were related to the needs of the pupils.

State agents for negro education in all the Southern States agree that the money spent by the Jeanes Fund and the counties for industrial supervision has produced more results per dollar than any money spent for negro education. The State of Virginia alone has 48 of these workers, many of them paid altogether from public funds.

The counties spent $10,505 in connection with the $5,995 secured from private funds. At the beginning of the year 1920, these 21 county workers were taken over by the agricultural extension department of the University of Arkansas. At present there are only nine negro home demonstration agents in the State. While some reduction in number was to be expected as a result of "hard times" and "economy," a loss of over half of the workers because of failure on the part of levying courts to provide local funds is a poor showing. If these workers had remained under the supervision of the rural school agent, perhaps less of the local money would have been lost. At present the State is not getting any help from the Jeanes Fund for negro schools. This is very unfortunate, to say the least.

Until other arrangements can be made, the Arkansas Extension Department should cooperate with the Jeanes Fund and rural school agent, using the State funds to match the Jeanes Fund. In this way this much-needed work can be reestablished in a number of counties.

The Slater Fund

The aid from the Slater Fund in Arkansas amounts to $4,750 a year. This money is used in the seven county training schools, at the rate of $500 a year, to pay all or part of the salary of the home-economics teacher. Two county training schools receive $100 a year for equipment. There are five town schools—Arkadelphia, Searcy, Crossett, Prescott, and Stuttgart—that receive aid from the Slater Fund for home economics. Arkadelphia receives $150, Searcy and Stuttgart $200 each, and Prescott and Crossett $250 each. This money is used to pay part of the salary of the home-economics teacher. The aid to the town schools is withdrawn at the rate of $50 a year so that the town board may gradually take over the home-economics work. In this way the Slater Fund's donation may be released and used elsewhere to establish a home-economics department.

The Rosenwald Fund

For the year ending December 30, 1921, the State department of education was offered $36,000 by the Rosenwald Fund for use in helping to build modern rural schoolhouses for negroes. The most important condition laid down was that the buildings should be *completed*, the money paid for the buildings after final inspection, and the reports sent in. The money became available July 1, 1920, so that in reality 18 months was allowed for the expenditure of this appropriation.

Of the $36,000 the sum of $19,000 was returned to the fund because it could not be used. A large number of applications were received, but the buildings were not erected, and some of the applications were transferred to the 1921–22 budget, which expired July 1, 1922. The State department expects to spend the entire appropriation covered by the 1921–22 budget, so that none of this money will be returned to the fund.

There were 18 school buildings in which Rosenwald aid from the 1920–21 budget was used. Four of these schools are of the one-teacher type; seven are of the two-teacher type; three are three-teacher buildings, and four were four-teacher buildings. The total cost of these buildings was $100,055; of this amount $76,007 was from public funds, $6,398 from colored people, and $16,300 from the Rosenwald Fund.

County Training Schools

There are nine county training schools in Arkansas. These institutions have been built in order that teachers might be trained in the counties where they live. These schools also serve to give high-school and vocational training to students expected to engage in other occupations. The aid of the Slater Fund, $500 a year, has promoted the teaching of home economics. The training in vocational agriculture, made possible by State and Federal funds, is a valuable feature of the school work at these schools. The Dallas County Training School at Fordyce is one of the best schools of this type in the State.

Part of the training given the boys and girls in this school is of immediate value to them. At the same time the traditional subjects in the course of study have not been neglected. The school furnishes a source of skilled and intelligent labor for Fordyce and Dallas County. The value of such an institution to both races is apparent to any one who sees the work that is actually being done.

Fear is sometimes expressed that the teaching of trades to the negroes will bring the race into economic competition with white workers and thereby cause trouble. Those who oppose trade training for negroes also oppose it for white youth, as these opponents have the idea of "limiting the output" so that a scarcity of skilled labor may result in an abnormal wage. But unless the industrial development of Arkansas is to be retarded, the vast amount of skilled work that must be done will provide employment for all. Opportunities will not be restricted for workers of either race. In Virginia and Alabama Hampton and Tuskegee Institutes have for years trained large numbers of colored mechanics. These tradesmen and those trained at the State agricultural and mechanical schools for negroes have migrated to every Southern State and engaged in skilled work. And yet industrial clashes have been almost unknown. This fact ought to be sufficient answer to those who claim that the vocational training of the negroes is a mistake.

Summary

The defects of the negro public schools of Arkansas may be summarized as follows:

(1) Of the negro population of school age, only 67.8 per cent are enrolled in school. If a larger percentage of the school population is to be enrolled, more facilities must be provided. At present the schools are not able to handle efficiently the pupils who are enrolled. Larger buildings are needed and more teachers. Even if the schools were 100 per

cent efficient, the money now being spent to maintain the schools is not sufficient to meet the situation.

(2) Of the pupils enrolled in the colored schools, only 66.2 per cent are in average attendance. The main causes of this are: (1) Poor teaching; (2) insanitary, uncomfortable, unattractive, and poorly equipped buildings; (3) course of study not sufficiently related to the everyday life of the child and his needs.

In order that the teaching may be improved, teachers should be paid according to their certificates, education, and experience. Summer schools must be provided if the teachers now in service are to make professional progress. The State should provide means for the training of an adequate number of teachers at the Agricultural, Mechanical, and Normal College at Pine Bluff, Ark. Better schoolhouses should be constructed. The Rosenwald plans and bills of material may be secured from the State department of education. Financial aid may be secured if these plans are used. These plans call for attractive, modern buildings, well lighted and ventilated, at a reasonable cost. State aid for buildings would make it possible for Arkansas to use more Rosenwald money. The course of study should include handicrafts, sewing, cooking, elementary manual training, and agriculture. This is especially true of the rural schools. These subjects can be introduced into the rural schools by industrial supervising teachers. These industrial supervisers can train the teachers as well as the pupils. In small schools there ought to be one qualified teacher who will give part of her time to this work. Larger schools, with five or more teachers, need at least one industrial teacher whose entire time is devoted to these subjects.

(3) The negro schools are suffering from a lack of supervision. The counties in Arkansas are large, and a county superintendent can not be expected to supervise, without help, all the white and colored schools in an average county. No business concern would spend $735,222 a year (the total cost of teaching negro children in Arkansas during the last school year) without spending a great deal more for supervision, management, direction, auditing, and general checking of results. It can not be assumed that money spent for public education is producing satisfactory results. The schools must have supervision so that the results of teaching may be checked up and the defects remedied. Each county superintendent needs a capable colored assistant to supervise the colored schools and, especially, to introduce industrial work into the schools.

(4) In many counties of Arkansas there is not a single school that can train teachers for rural schools. A large increase in the number of county training schools would remedy this situation to a considerable extent. There should be some supply of teachers in each county. In addition to training teachers, the county training schools can give boys and girls the

combination of high-school education and vocational training—in other words, "education for life." The State could encourage the building of the schools by aiding those that maintain satisfactory standards.

(5) Rural education presents a difficult problem at best, but there is no good reason why the negro school facilities in some of the towns of Arkansas should not be greatly improved. Negro children can not be educated for one-fourth what it costs to educate white children.

(6) Even with good teachers, suitable buildings, and ample equipment the schools can not be efficient if there are more than 35 pupils to the teacher. Under the most favorable conditions, a ratio of 50 pupils per teacher means that the children will be two-thirds taught, and a ratio of 70 pupils per teacher means that they will be half taught.

(7) A graded school is more efficient than one that is not graded. The closer a school comes to being graded, the more efficient it is. As a rule the average one or two teacher school is not efficient because of the large number of recitations the teacher must hear every day. There are too many one and two teacher negro schools in Arkansas. Many of these could be eliminated by consolidation. More large schools with three or more teachers would mean increased efficiency. (63–74)

COUNTY TRAINING SCHOOLS

The discussions under the subheadings "State Supervision of Schools," "The Jeanes Fund," "The Slater Fund," "The Rosenwald Fund," and "County Training Schools" in the preceding document show that northern foundations had a significant impact on African American schools. In his article "Northern Foundations and the Shaping of Southern Black Rural Education, 1902–1935," James D. Anderson describes the philosophy of the early educational reformers at the turn of the century: "[Robert C.] Ogden, [George Foster] Peabody, and [William H.] Baldwin [Jr.] were the key spokesmen for a larger group of philanthropic reformers who were particularly interested in industrial education as a means of training efficient and contented black laborers for the Southern agricultural economy" (374). These reformers presented their ideas to the Rockefeller family, and eventually the General Education Board (GEB) was founded in 1902. Anderson details the programs sponsored by the GEB:

In pursuit of its goal to develop industrial education in Southern black schools and hence to retain blacks as efficient agricultural and domestic workers in rural society, the General Education Board initiated and sustained some extraordinarily active and far-reaching programs. Beginning around 1910, the GEB penetrated the Southern educational structure with three major programs: the establishment of State Supervisors for Negro Rural Schools in all the Southern states; the placing of County Supervising Industrial Teachers (commonly known as the Jeanes Teachers) in hundreds of Southern counties; and the development of *County Training Schools, the most important mechanism for translating the GEB's educational concerns into institutional action at the local level* [emphasis added]. These programs, funded by the GEB, the John F. Slater Fund and the Anna T. Jeanes Fund, significantly determined the forms of education available to Southern blacks during the first half of the twentieth century. (381)

Evidence of the success of the northern foundations' programs in Arkansas is clear in the analysis provided in the preceding document. By 1923 each of the three major programs cited above had taken root in the state in some form.

Angelou's description of her eighth-grade graduation from Lafayette County Training School demonstrates, however, that the goals of white reformers were not necessarily those of African Americans themselves. Angelou portrays her pride in her academic accomplishments, and her subsequent despair and bitterness when Edward Donleavy, a white man invited to deliver the commencement address at her graduation, first describes the forthcoming improvements at the local white school (a visiting artist and new scientific equipment) and then what the African American students can look forward to: a paved playing field and perhaps some new equipment for the home economics and workshop facilities. Angelou clearly does not agree with the emphasis on vocational training endorsed by Donleavy and the northern foundations, and neither did many other African Americans, as James D. Anderson notes in *The Education of Blacks in the South, 1860–1935*:

Although the philanthropists found it relatively easy to sell the idea of the county training school to the state supervisors, it was quite another task to sell it to the black people of the rural South. . . . [T]he state supervisors encountered opposition from rural black principals and teachers from the outset. In 1913 Favrot stated privately that rural black teachers' opposition to industrial training made it extremely difficult to introduce industrial education into the black rural schools of Arkansas. Four years later, John A. Presson, who succeeded Favrot as state supervisor of Arkansas, gained some insight into the underlying causes of the black teachers' resistance to industrial education. He visited the state's black colleges where a good portion of them had been educated. Presson discovered that the three black colleges—Philander Smith, Arkansas Baptist, and Shorter—were "not equipped at all, for teaching industrial subjects." Moreover, "they seem to pride themselves on their academic work, and take great credit to themselves for work offered in traditional courses, such as are given by leading colleges of the country." Because these colleges had in attendance "a considerable number of students who are planning to teach in the schools of the state," Presson was anxious to convert them to a more favorable view of industrial education. He was not very successful in this effort. (141–42)

In the next document, Edward Redcay explores the early beginnings of the county training schools, their development, purposes, and characteristics, and their place in the Arkansas school system. Redcay defines county training schools as "those larger public county schools for Negroes in the Southern states which are open in the higher grades to children from all parts of the county, and offering, or planning to offer, work including the eighth grade or higher, and which have been aided by the John F. Slater Fund" (12–13).

It is interesting to note in the first excerpt that, in contrast to Anderson's findings, it is an African American principal who asks for aid in developing a program in agriculture for the boys and domestic sciences for the girls. Hence, African American attitudes toward the necessity and usefulness of county training schools were not monolithic, but rather varied according to the needs and philosophies of the parties involved.

EDWARD E. REDCAY, *COUNTY TRAINING SCHOOLS AND PUBLIC SECONDARY EDUCATION FOR NEGROES IN THE SOUTH* (1935)
(Reprint. Westport, Conn.: Negro Universities Press, 1970)

The Development of County Training Schools in the South

The facts which led to the establishment of one of the first of these schools tell a story of wider significance than the specific school situation itself.

On April 9, 1910, Professor A. M. Strange, B.S., the Negro principal of the Graded School in Collins, Mississippi, wrote to Dr. James H. Dillard, the general agent of the Slater Fund and President of the Anna T. Jeanes Foundation, for assistance in the employment of an industrial teacher for the girls. "The aim of the school is to specialize two lines of work, viz: Scientific Agriculture for the boys and the domestic sciences for the girls. Hence the import of this letter to you is asking aid in the interest of the girls."

By September of the same year, Strange had left Collins, Mississippi, for he wrote next from Kentwood, Louisiana. This time he was soliciting aid for a school to be known as the "Kentwood A. and I. Institute." Evidently, Dr. Dillard was interested in the idea, for on November 17, 1910, Strange wrote a letter, part of which will be quoted. It eloquently reveals the growing economic problems of the races and the cooperative means through which the early movement for public secondary schools for Negroes gained impetus. Part of the original letter in uncorrected form is quoted below:

"... I note from the tone of your letter that you are deeply interested in our welfare. These is but one hope for the Negro, as a mass in the Southland, and that hope is to have him imbibe and inculcate the idea of going back to the farm and there make good. We see daily, facts demonstrated concerning the negro in the trades. Since the northern white mechanics have come into the southland with their unionized system of labor, painting, carpentry, brickmasonary and various other bread winning persuits which go to make up a working man's support in the city are now being closed to the negro, it is only a question of time when the negro as an entiety will be counted out of the trade life of the city. With above stated facts we naturally conclude that the best form which will send him with head, heart and hand trained, back to farm buy small plats of land build good homes cultivate their 10 or 12 acres persue the tenor of their way and make substantial progress.

"We have succeeded in interesting the good white people of this section of parish and parish board of education to help us put the before mentioned idea into execution. This school fosters the idea of having boys learn scientific agriculture, dairying and horticulture for girls sewing, domestic economy, cooking, dairying and poultry raising." ... (26–27)

In the establishment of these first County Training Schools no one pattern was carried out. In each instance it was fundamentally a problem of local adaptation to be worked out through a variety of cooperative sources involving both races. There were, however, several common factors in each situation.

1. A recognized need for a bigger and better school to offer to Negroes in the county or parish a more advanced education than that afforded by the rural elementary schools.
2. The recognition of the need for better prepared teachers for the county or parish.
3. The frequent mention of agricultural and industrial education.
4. The willingness to cooperate in order to secure the support of a philanthropic organization. (30)

Aims and Purposes of County Training Schools

Since there were no precedents to follow in encouraging the development of these schools, the spread of the idea to other states and counties necessitated some determination of their aims and purposes to lend direction to the efforts of the schools already established and those to follow.

At a meeting of State Agents ["State Agents" are agents for Negro education in the Southern States] and others interested in Negro education, a committee consisting of Messrs. Leo M. Favrot, James L. Sibley, and Jackson Davis was appointed to set forth the general aims and purposes of County Training Schools, and to formulate a suggested course of study for these schools. After several meetings wherein the opinions of county school boards, state departments of education, and the philanthropic groups assisting in the establishment and maintenance of these schools were considered, the following aims and purposes were presented:

1. "To supply for the county a central Negro public training school offering work two or three years in advance of that offered by the common schools.

2. "To establish a type of Negro school in the county which shall serve as a model with respect to physical plant and equipment, teaching force, course of study, and plan of operation.

3. "To lay emphasis on thorough work in all common school studies, to relate these studies to the lives of the pupils, and to develop standards of achievement.

4. "To give industrial training, laying particular emphasis upon subjects pertaining to home and farm.

5. "To prepare Negro boys and girls to make a good living and lead a useful life by knowing how to care for the home, to utilize land, to make home gardens, to raise their own meat, poultry products, milk products, etc.

6. "To prepare young men and young women to become rural and elementary school teachers, by enabling them to meet legal requirements of the state, by giving them a close acquaintance and sympathy with rural activities, and by supplying such elementary professional training as will help them to secure the best results in this work. The need in the South for properly qualified Negro rural teachers is everywhere apparent."

In short, the purpose of the County Training School was to offer a more advanced education, based upon a necessary adaptation to the demands of rural life and to the training of teachers for the rural schools within the county. (33, 35)

Characteristics of County Training Schools

The large majority of County Training Schools were, in their early days, somewhat larger elementary schools located in rural areas wherein the Negro population tended to be dense. Frequently the smaller neighboring elementary schools were absorbed into these larger and more centrally located schools. While certain of them offered some secondary work at the time they were selected to serve as Training Schools, most of them had to evolve gradually to high school status. As the demand for more advanced education increased and means for providing it were made available, the secondary grades were added. Today in many counties in the South this same developmental cycle is in process in County Training Schools. In practically every case the enrollment is largely centered in the elementary grades. The sizes of these schools vary tremendously, ranging from slightly more than 100 pupils to well over 800. The average Training School in 1933 possessed a student body numbering 300 students, of which 46 were to be found in the secondary grades. From this general account it can be seen that these schools represent a som[e]what unusual type of consolidated school development.

Some of the schools which are located in the larger urban communities have tended to develop along conventional American high school lines. On the other hand, the large majority, which are located in the open country or in small rural places, tend to adapt their educational offerings to the needs of the rural constituencies they are intended to serve. The attempt to aid the rural Negro is reflected in many ways. Practically all Training Schools offer instructional and laboratory facilities in the agricultural, industrial, and domestic sciences. These services are usually made available to both students and adults residing in the county. Invariably the "Smith-Hughes-teacher" is placed in these schools, and not infrequently he serves as the principal of the school. In attempting to make these schools more available to students from distant parts of the county, dormitories are at times included as part of the physical plant. In 1927 there were 66 Training schools possessing dormitory facilities for students. The problem of providing suitable living accommodations for teachers is nowhere more serious than in connection with Negro rural schools. Teachers' homes were included as part of the plant in 98 schools in 1927. Because so many of these schools are the largest or the only secondary schools in the counties wherein they are located, much of the community, social and general activity of the Negro population centers in them. Efforts to harmonize the interests of County Training Schools and the communities which they serve have in many cases met with marked success.

A better conception of the general nature of these schools can be gained from a description of several of them. While the following examples naturally are not typical of all of these schools, they give a general impression of the physical set-up, and show what is being done in some of them. The data presented below are taken from records which were made by the author while visiting schools on a field trip.

Warren County Training School, Wise, North Carolina

This county is inhabited by 23,000 persons, of whom 15,000 are Negroes. Two schools offer secondary work—the County Training School and the J. R. Hawkins High School at Warrenton. Each school serves, roughly, half of the county. Largely through the financial efforts of the Negroes themselves and the Rosenwald fund, fifteen buses have been secured. With the exception of a small section of the county possessing only paths for roads, every section can offer the Negro youth an opportunity for high school educational facilities at public expense. This county serves as an excellent example of what can be done in providing transportation.

The County Training School is located in the open country. The physical plant consists of an eleven-room brick building erected in 1931 to replace a frame structure destroyed by a tornado; one four-room frame structure housing the seventh grade and the elementary school library; another frame building wherein the agricultural, industrial, and domestic science classes are conducted; a combination dormitory and teachers' home; the principal's house, and several small frame structures which were erected by the boys in the manual training courses. These buildings house farm machinery, cattle, pigs, chickens, etc.

A staff of five teachers and the principal conduct the educational offerings in the secondary grades. One of these teachers is the "Smith-Hughes teacher," who has charge of the industrial and agricultural work conducted in the school and in the neighboring county. The student body approximates 300 persons, of whom about half are found in the high school grades. This secondary enrollment is somewhat higher than that usually found in a Training School of this size. The main building has a large auditorium, which seats 350 persons comfortably. A fine secondary school library is also housed in this building. The work of the school is fully accredited by the State Department of Education.

Some idea of the school-community relationship can be sensed from the following account of this type of activity. Prior to 1929, the Negroes in this county raised largely cotton and tobacco crops. When the depression set in, few of these farmers re-directed their efforts toward producing crops which would be of use in daily living. With the cotton and tobacco markets virtually closed to them much poverty and suffering resulted. In 1929 Mr. Cheek, principal of the school, with his staff and others, initiated a campaign to persuade Negro farmers to raise corn, wheat, cattle, pigs, and chickens on a scale large enough to supply the Negro citizenry with food. Sufficient money was raised to purchase modern farm machinery. This was sent out from the School and used cooperatively by the farmers. The first year three families raised 4,500 bushels of wheat. One Negro started a flour mill. Negro farmers now cooperate in using this machinery and do much corn-cutting, threshing, etc., for white farmers. With the money raised, they have purchased a pedigreed bull, several fine breeding hogs, and fine Leghorn and Rhode Island Red chicken breeders. All are kept at the school and tended by students. All are used cooperatively by the farmers. Adult classes are offered at the school, and garden and poultry projects are conducted by students at their homes. From what has been described it can be seen that this school is, literally, the farm center for the county.

The Montgomery County Training School, Waugh, Alabama

This county is inhabited by 98,000 persons, of whom 52,000 are Negroes. Two schools in Montgomery (City) offer two years of high school work to negroes. The County Training School is the only one in the entire county offering four years of secondary work. Little or no transportation is provided.

This school is located in the open country, with the surrounding area populated almost entirely by Negroes, and is about twelve miles from the nearest city, Montgomery. Four frame buildings constitute the major portion of the physical plant. This plant consists of the main school building, the domestic and vocational science building, and two frame dwellings occupied by the teaching staff and boarding students. The grounds have been nicely landscaped and are clean and well-kept. The main drive has been named after Dr. Dillard, former president of the Slater Fund, and Lambert Walk has been named for one of the present State Agents for Negro Education. The buildings have no central heating plants, no running water, and all toilet facilities are out-of-doors. Electricity is supplied by a plant on the grounds, which was secured through the cooperative efforts of the Negroes themselves. Several smaller sheds and buildings house farm implements, cattle, pigs, chickens and mules. Several acres of gardens and fields are part of the school property.

The school is organized on the 6–3-3 plan, and has enrolled 325 pupils, of whom 85 are in the secondary grades. The principal, who holds the M.A. degree from Harvard, and three additional teachers provide the instruction in the secondary grades. The school is accredited for three of the four years of high school work that is offered. One senses a fine attitude of cooperation about this school. Modern progressive techniques are employed, especially in the lower elementary grades. Here, however, general over-crowding prevails and limits the extent to which these techniques can be applied.

All the girls wear colored cotton dresses, which have been made in the domestic science classes. This is not designed as an attempt to provide uniforms, but rather as a matter of practical economy both for school use and in the home. The material is durable, washable, inexpensive and not easily soiled. Adult women attend classes and learn, among other things, to make these dresses.

At the time the writer visited the school the "Smith-Hughes teacher" was conducting a class in Biology. A practical lesson was in session. A pig, raised at the school, had just been slaughtered by the boys, under the guidance of their instructor. In a short time they were joined by the girls of the class and the entire group proceeded to study the animal. The teacher used every opportunity to have each member of the group participate in this real-laboratory situation wherein the details of external and internal bodily structure and the functions of certain organs of a mammal could be studied more effectively than would have been possible in an ordinary classroom.

After the boys had attended to the details of cutting and dressing the pig, the girls aided in cleaning and preparing the utensils to be used in lard, sausages, etc. Throughout the entire project it was obvious that the instructor was using this common-place rural activity,—conducted in a practical, sanitary, and economical manner,—as a medium for vitalized learning.

These two examples are illustrative of County Training Schools which have been thus identified for ten or more years. The success of their work is largely a reflection of wise administrative guidance on the part of the principal and local and state officials. The Slater Fund has played a minor part in providing stimulative funds and, in the earlier history of these schools, some advisory assistance.

The final example to be submitted concerns a school in an early developmental stage. It is indicative of many County Training Schools in their formative stages.

The Spotsylvania County Training School, Snell, Virginia

This county is inhabited by 10,000 persons, of whom 3,000 are Negroes. In addition, it should be mentioned that the population of Fredericksburg city, which has a political autonomy entirely separate from that of the county, aggregates 7,000 persons, of whom 1,200 are Negroes.

The Mayfield High School is located in this city and offers four years of secondary work to Negroes.

The Spotsylvania County Training School is fifty-odd miles from Washington, D.C. The school was formerly owned by a Board representing several denominational interests. It has been turned over to the county. In addition to the solitary building, the school grounds include 250 acres of land, much of which is covered with timber. The building is a crude, frame, barnlike structure containing a basement and two floors. Six rooms on the first floor are used for classrooms, and the second floor serves as living quarters for the teaching staff and several boarding students from Louisa county. There is no central heating plant, each room being supplied with a small "cannonball" stove; no electricity; no running water; and a single outside toilet serves the entire school. The grounds and building quite obviously needed renovating.

The school offers four years of high school work, and of the 200 pupils 48 were enrolled in the secondary grades. One part-time teacher and two full-time teachers present the high school subjects. The science equipment represents the bare minimum essentials. There were too few seats for the pupils, and very few text books and supplies seemed to be available for student use. There was no "Smith-Hughes teacher" placed in this school and consequently no agricultural work was offered. The principal, Mr. Duncan, is a graduate of Tuskegee Institute, Alabama, and, while able to offer the manual training, could not teach the agricultural courses. It was the principal's first year at this school. He was working hard to secure community interest and cooperation, and reported that his greatest obstacle was to overcome the lack of parental interest in the work of the school. He was trying to raise $200 in order to bring the school library up to the standards set by the state. The work of this school is not accredited.

These examples are not entirely representative of County Training Schools wherever they are found. They do, however, give some concrete factual information which should facilitate more intelligent appreciation of what these schools are and how they function. In the last example it should be seen that much remains to be accomplished in bringing this school to a satisfactory status.

A final caution is necessary for those who are not familiar with Negro schools as they are found in the Southern states. There are some splendidly equipped and well staffed schools for Negroes in the South. Unfortunately they constitute a far too inadequate minority and are too largely available only to an urban population. The great majority of Negroes must resort to far less impressive educational agencies than those just mentioned. Frame buildings, frequently outmoded and wornout, without central heating plants, without running water, without electricity, and with outside toilet accommodations are the rule. County Training Schools are no exception to this general type, except that they are usually larger and somewhat better equipped. Schools offering elementary work are invariably badly over-crowded, especially in the first three grades. There is an appalling dearth of text books, and many of those in use are in poor condition or poorly adapted to the students who are supposed to use them. The same scarcity applies to teaching materials. Both of these insufficiencies are due largely to the fact that the majority of Southern states do not supply these items free of charge. When it is recalled that the South as a whole compares unfavorably with the per capita wealth of other sections of the United States, a further reason is seen for this educational poverty. And in these Southern states, the Negro, more often than not, is the poorest of the poor. Finally, one must bear in mind the fact that in the allocation of public monies for educational purposes, a discrimination is practiced to the disadvantage of the Negro, which is exceedingly adroit, if not downright dishonest. (45–50)

The Place of County Training Schools in the Secondary Field

Great variability characterizes the percentages indicative of the extent to which Negroes in the several states sought their only, or most advanced, public high school education in County Training Schools. Arkansas with 71.7 per cent presented one extreme and Maryland, with 3.6 per cent, the other. In general those states having the greater Negro population seem to depend most upon the secondary function discharged through the Training Schools. The conspicuous exceptions to this tendency are Arkansas, Florida and Kentucky, with relatively small Negro populations and high percentages of dependency upon County Training Schools; and North Carolina and Texas, with large Negro populations and less dependency upon these schools. . . .

Arkansas

Arkansas enrolled but 6.9 per cent of its total estimated Negro secondary population in 1933, while seven states with substantially larger Negro population enrolled larger percentages. It has been shown that this state had 57.9 per cent of its Negro population living in counties offering *less* than four years of secondary work. This is a higher percentage than any other Southern state yielded. . . . Despite the fact that 80 per cent of the Negro population is rural, there were but five four-year public secondary schools located in non-urban centers. Of the 36 schools identified at some time as County Training Schools, ten offer four-year secondary programs, and only two of these are located in rural communities. The facts indicate a most unfavorable situation as far as Negro secondary educables are concerned.

Several factors, the relative importance of which cannot be accurately estimated, could be responsible. The area of counties would seem important. Other states, however, have equally large counties and seem to provide more adequately for Negro secondary pupils. Transportation of pupils is another consideration. It appears that few Negro students are transported. This aggravates the rural student's predicament. State control through supervision and high school classification is another conditioning aspect. The facts indicate that much local autonomy is effective. The State authorities classify secondary schools only at the request or invitation of the local school authorities. Provision is made for accrediting schools as 6–3, 6–4, 6–6, 6–3-3, 8–3, 8–2, and 8–4 organizations, thereby allowing for much variation.

The status of the county superintendency is decidedly problematical, with that office being, at least temporarily, abolished. In addition, the entire program of instruction, and consequently, of organization, is undergoing a change. These recent changes, while important, have hardly been responsible for what seems to be a cumulative condition in Negro secondary education.

The County Training School movement has been active in Arkansas for 22 years. An average of 8.5 years aid to a county characterizes the distribution for all counties assisted since 1911. The fact that 71.7 per cent of the Negroes of high school age who were in counties providing some secondary work in 1933, resided in counties wherein County Training Schools offered most of that which constituted public secondary education—is testimony to the Training School's importance to the minority race. On the other hand, the fact that only ten Training Schools offered four years of secondary work, and only two of these were in rural localities, indicates a development not entirely consistent with comparative developmental tendencies evidenced in other states. (85–87)

ATTITUDES OF AFRICAN AMERICANS
TOWARD EDUCATION

Angelou's description of her reaction to Edward Donleavy's speech at her graduation clearly demonstrates her personal opposition to Donleavy's belief that African Americans might only aspire to be athletes, domestics, or manual laborers. From her remarks one can also infer that Angelou's teachers were among those who took pride in their academic work and who challenged and undermined the agenda of white philanthropists from the North.

The following excerpt from Charles S. Johnson's *Growing Up in the Black Belt* further explores the attitudes of African Americans toward education by providing firsthand accounts of their views. Johnson identifies two primary themes in the remarks of those interviewed: first, parents see the practical need for their children to become literate so that they may avoid being cheated; and second, education is seen to provide an alternative to life as a farmer.

CHARLES S. JOHNSON, *GROWING UP IN THE BLACK BELT:
NEGRO YOUTH IN THE RURAL SOUTH*
(Washington, D.C.: American Council on Education, 1941)

Attitudes Toward Education

The results of our study indicate that the presumed practical values of education have become a motivating force for both parents and children to a remarkable degree, even in the plantation area. Their reasons were varied. Some wanted an education so they could "live in town," some "to make a living." One boy said, "Everybody needs to know how to read and count." The increased possibility of securing desirable work was perhaps most common. A 12-year-old seventh-grade Johnston County, North Carolina, girl, whose family is economically well-off according to community standards, thought, "Everybody ought to go to school and get educated. If you get a heap of schooling you get plenty of jobs when you finish." A 17-year-old tenth-grade Shelby County, boy said:

I like school just fine because it tells you how to do the right thing at the right time. An education will tell you whether to farm this year or to do something else.

From this same area another youth expressed the view that:

> An education is good to have. You might get a job in Clayton and
> you will have to know how to count and you can make better
> change.

Although many reasons for their interest in "schooling" were given, in
general, education appears to have two vital meanings for most of these
youth and their parents. First, education makes people literate. These
people believe that their poverty is largely attributable to their inability
to read and write. Hence, for them education meets an immediate, practical need. It protects them against frauds often practiced upon ignorant
people who are tenant farmers.

A Johnston County, North Carolina, farmer of high standing in the
community explained the attitude of parents who themselves had not
had extensive education:

> I didn't get far, but I am anxious for my children to remain in school
> until they finish high school at least. I would like for them to attend
> college. I intend to send them, too, if my health keeps up. Children
> need plenty of education these days so they can go into business
> without folks cheating them.

A Bolivar County, Mississippi, tenant farmer said:

> Children need all the education they can get and ought to get
> enough to keep people from cheating them. They should go
> through high school, and farther if they can. Especially the boys;
> they is the ones that need the education, 'cause they has to make
> a living.

Secondly, education is regarded as a means of escape from the pros-
pect of an unpleasant occupation which is frequently associated in the
minds of Negroes with a low racial status. The hope that education may
offer a way of escape is expressed by a deserted, sharecropper mother of
six children:

> I plan to let the children keep on in school as long as they want,
> until they want to leave. It sure is hard, but I'm willin' to struggle
> along to help them all I can. If a child ain't got a good education
> now days it be mighty hard on them. If I'd a had more of it I
> wouldn't be so hard put now. I went to the sixth and had to come
> out to work. I don't know nothin' but farmin' and it's hard makin'
> a livin' on the farm. My girl is the oldest and I'm goin' to help her
> stay in school. She's smart, too.

A 16-year-old eighth-grade plantation girl of Macon County, Alabama, commented:

> I'd rather go to school than farm. I really like school. My folks are going to try and send me to Tuskegee and I want to go, too. It costs a lot of money and I can't say I'll get to go, but I sure do want to go, for I'd rather do anything than farm, and if I go to school I can do something else.

Another youth said, "Everybody ought to have an education. If you don't have an education, you'll have to work on a farm all the time." A 12-year-old fifth-grader remarked:

> If it weren't for schools Negroes would be in a terrible shape. If there weren't any schools, Negroes wouldn't know anything and would have to always work on the farm.

A mother in a Madison County, Alabama, tenant family, living nine miles from the nearest school, further illustrates the escape aspect of education when, speaking of her daughter, she says:

> 'Cose there ain't much for a girl this far in the country, but we get on pretty good. We been so anxious for her to get her schooling we just pay a man $2.50 a month. He picks her up and a few others on the highway ever' morning. I wants to see her keep getting educated. I didn't go no higher than the fifth grade or I'd not be here on a farm today. I sho' don't intend for her to have to work on no farm.

A Macon County, Alabama, mother, viewing education as the chief avenue of occupational escape said:

> I didn't get very high in school, went to 'bout the sixth grade. My husband, he only went as far as the fourth. I had to come out and help my folks farm and just didn't get back. I wants all these children to get all the education they can. They ought to finish high school and that's what we be planning on—sending them to high school and college, too, if they hold out and stay in school. Trouble is, today most young folks don't want no schooling. All they want is a good time. I say you got to have education now to get a job what will pay any money.

Apparently no sacrifices were too great for the majority of the parents to make in order to secure for their children the advantages of an education. A widowed domestic day worker in Davidson County, Tennessee, said:

I want Bennie to stay in school just as long as I am able to send her. That's why I sent her out there to the boarding school. Like it be with me working out, girls can get into so much trouble and I felt that out there she would be watched over and be learning all at once. It takes all I can make, for ain't nobody to keep the children but me, but I want Bennie to get learning.

In this same vein, another widow from Macon County said:

I want my girls to finish high school. I'll send them as long as I can, but I can't tell how long I'll be able to keep them. It's right high [expensive] sending children to school and boarding them out, but I want them to get some learning.

Some parents are so solicitous of their children's welfare that they personally supervise their educational progress. One Shelby County, Tennessee, farmer said:

Every year when school opens I goes down to the school and see his new teacher. I tell her what I want my son to learn and how I want him to act. My boy is a good student; he gets his lesson fine. If something goes wrong at school I goes down and see what the trouble is.

Other parents make no attempt to hide their disgust or sorrow when their children lack interest in school. A Bolivar County, Mississippi, resident spoke strongly of his son's lack of interest in school.

I don't know what is the matter with that blockhead. Me and his mother done everything for him, but he just won't do no good. He ain't been near no school for three years and he's 17 now. I just wish I had the opportunity he had when I was coming along. The world expects more of him than it does of people like me. I'm going down and he's coming up, but he won't go to school.

The wife of a Macon County, Alabama, farmer of moderate circumstances said proudly:

Our daughter wants to try and go to Selma University, down here at Selma, and her father will sure try to send her, too. If he halfway got the money and she really want to go, he'll sure send her.

In some cases, even after the child had married, the parents still wished to have the process of formal education continued. One sharecropping widow in Coahoma County, Mississippi, who had four daughters said:

I wanted Baby to finish her schooling. I wanted her to go all the way. I went to Tuskegee in 1925 on a visit. I wanted Baby to go to school there. It don't make no difference about her being married. I want her to go there if she don't do nothing but learn a trade and then she will be able to take care of herself. Lots of people go to school after they are married. Sometimes they do better because their mind is settled.

Although the hostile, indifferent "folk" attitudes toward education are rapidly giving way in the face of new conditions, need for the children's labor not infrequently is rationalized in terms of a lack of need for education. This attitude appeared most frequently in areas within the shadow of the plantation. An interesting example of this attitude appears in the comment of a struggling, illiterate sharecropper in Bolivar County who has seven children, all but one of whom are illiterate.

I ain't so worried 'bout my children getting all this schooling. They ain't going to do nothing nohow but work on the farm. I'll send them upon consideration up to the sixth grade, then they got to come out and help me. I went as high as the seventh, but it didn't do me no good. Unless you can go on to college, schooling ain't no 'count. My children just as well be home as chasing over there to that school house wastin' time and money.

The child's reaction to this attitude was both wistful and pathetic:

I like school. I always want to stay in school, but I reckon after this year I can't. Maw thinks I am big enough to stay home and work, and schooling costs so much. Sometimes I dream that when I am bigger I am going off and finish school, sometimes it seems like I am away at school.

A rationalization for her failure to attend school, presented by an 18-year-old Coahoma County girl who had been married for three years, combines a disrespect for the value of education in plantation life and for the school facilities that are available to Negroes:

Education is all right for those who wants it for somethin' they want to do. If you gonna farm all your life, though, you jus' wastin' your time goin' to school. And that's what most of 'em gonna do. Dey gonna stay right here on some of these plantations all their life anyhow. Colored school ain't near 'bout doin' much good nohow. They open way late after the white school done opened and dey close up 'fore the white schools shut down. Now how's school gonna do any good if you can't stay there as long as you oughta?

Further disapproval of modern education is voiced by a Bolivar County parent who said:

I believe education is like this: If it prepares you to do something, then it's all right. Now, I believe a person ought to go as far as the eighth grade. After that he ought to take a trade—bricklayin' or plasterin' or something he can work at with his hands. All those people you see 'round Clarksdale and in the city what done finished up, walkin' 'round holdin' their hands, with nothing to do. What's the use of learnin' how to be a bookkeeper if you ain't gonna never have no books to keep? That ain't for no niggers. (114–19)

STUDY QUESTIONS

1. In what specific ways did segregation affect the quality of schools for African Americans in the South? in Arkansas? In your answers, be sure to discuss the differences between white and black schools.

2. Describe a typical African American elementary school in the south before desegregation. Include size and description of the facility and of the classroom(s), number of students per class, distribution of students through the grades, availability and condition of books and equipment, and so on.

3. Describe a typical African American teacher in a southern elementary school before desegregation. Discuss salary, preparation for teaching, and so on.

4. What do you think were the most important indicators of the state of education in Arkansas as described by the 1923 survey? What were the most important recommendations for change?

5. Summarize the history of the development of county training schools and the goals northern foundations set for these schools.

6. How important were the county training schools in Arkansas in 1923? in 1935 (according to Redcay's study)?

7. What common characteristics exist among the three county training schools described by Redcay: Warren County Training School, Montgomery County Training School, and Spotsylvania County Training School?

8. What reasons do some African American parents and children offer in favor of education? What reasons do others give against education?

TOPICS FOR WRITTEN OR ORAL EXPLORATION

1. How would you evaluate the curriculum at the African American school in Dine Hollow described by Charles S. Johnson in *Growing Up in the Black Belt*? What conditions there prevent the students from receiving a better education? What conditions prevent the teacher from doing a more effective job? How do the conditions at Dine Hollow compare to those found at your school?

2. What kinds of programs did the northern foundations support, and what motivated them to do so? What is your opinion of the programs? Explain your answer.

3. Write a dialogue between an agent of a Northern foundation and a typical African American teacher or parent.

4. Compare what you know about Angelou's school, as revealed in *I Know Why the Caged Bird Sings* with the typical African American school described in this chapter. Which of the three county training schools described in detail by Redcay do you think Angelou's school most closely resembled? Why?

5. Write a dialogue between two African American parents who express contrasting views regarding the education of their children.

6. How does Redcay's evaluation of the county training schools differ from the analysis offered by James D. Anderson? (Anderson's works are quoted in the introductory comments on county training schools in this chapter.)

7. Compare and contrast the attitude toward education expressed by Charlie Holcomb in "Tech 'Er Off, Charlie" (Chapter 2) with those expressed by African American parents in this chapter.

8. From your reading of *I Know Why the Caged Bird Sings*, what were Angelou's family's values regarding education? What were Angelou's own views as a child?

9. After reading this chapter, do you think efforts to desegregate the schools were justified? Why or why not?

WORKS CITED

Anderson, James D. *The Education of Blacks in the South, 1860–1935*. Chapel Hill: University of North Carolina Press, 1988.

————."Northern Foundations and the Shaping of Southern Black Rural Education, 1902–1935." *History of Education Quarterly* (Winter 1978): 371–96.

Angelou, Maya. *I Know Why the Caged Bird Sings*. 1970. Toronto: Bantam Books, 1971.

Foster, Emery M. *Statistical Summary of Education, 1939–40*. Vol. 2. Washington, D.C.: GPO, 1943.

Johnson, Harry A. "Public Education: The Battle and Its Aftermath." In *Negotiating the Mainstream*. Ed. Harry A. Johnson. Chicago: American Library Association, 1978. 1–46.

Pierce, Truman M., et al. *White and Negro Schools in the South: An Analysis of Biracial Education*. Englewood Cliffs, N.J.: Prentice-Hall, 1955.

Plessy vs. Ferguson. 163 U.S. 537, 16 S. Ct. 1138 (1896).

SUGGESTED READINGS

See the full text of works excerpted in this chapter.

The Guide to American Law: Everyone's Legal Encyclopedia. St. Paul: West, 1984.

Johnson, Ben F. III. " 'All Thoughtful Citizens': The Arkansas School Reform Movement, 1921–1930." *Arkansas Historical Quarterly* 46 (Summer 1987): 105–32.

Presson, J. A. "Annual Report of Educational Activities in Negro Schools." *Bulletin: State of Arkansas Department of Education*. Year Ending June 30, 1923. Found in Special Collections Division, University of Arkansas Libraries, Fayetteville.

Raper, Arthur. *Preface to Peasantry: A Tale of Two Black Belt Counties*. 1936. Reprint. New York: Atheneum, 1968.

Stinnett, T. M., and Clara B. Kennan. *All This and Tomorrow Too*. Little Rock: Arkansas Education Association, 1969.

Swift, Fletcher Harper. "The Public School System of Arkansas: Report of a Survey Made under the Direction of the United States Commissioner of Education at the Request of the Arkansas State Educational Commission. Part II." *Bulletin*. 1923, 11. Washington, D.C.: GPO, 1923.

Thomas, David Y. *Arkansas and Its People: A History, 1541–1930*. Vol. 2. New York: The American Historical Society, 1930.

4

The African American Church

Many scholars who have studied the African American Church agree that it is the institution that has had the greatest impact on the African American community. Many slaves were first introduced to Christianity on the southern plantations. The church was a source of comfort and inspiration to them as they endured the horrifying conditions of slavery. The institution continues to provide solace to African Americans in the face of racism, violence, and poverty and has been a unifying force in the community.

The African American church has played a major role in rural communities. In 1933 Mays and Nicholson reported that "three-quarters of all Negro churches are rural" (238). Certainly the church was a major force in Maya Angelou's life in the rural community of Stamps. It is no accident that the opening scene of *I Know Why the Caged Bird Sings* takes place in church. Indeed, Maya and her family seem to have devoted a great deal of time to church and church-related activities. In *Singin' and Swingin' and Gettin' Merry Like Christmas*, the third volume of her autobiography, Angelou writes:

> I had grown up in a Christian Methodist Episcopal Church where my uncle was superintendent of Sunday School, and my grand-mother was Mother of the Church. Until I was thirteen and left

Arkansas for California, each Sunday I spent a minimum of six hours in church. Monday evenings Momma took me to Usher Board Meeting; Tuesdays the Mothers of the Church met; Wednesday was for prayer meeting; Thursday, the Deacons congregated; Fridays and Saturdays were spent in preparation for Sunday. (13)

Maya's grandmother is fiercely religious, and her religious convictions are a sustaining force in her life. As a Mother of the Church, "an honorific title usually reserved for the wife of the founder or for the oldest and most respected members" (Lincoln and Mamiya, 275), Momma's religious authority is recognized. She begins each day on her knees in prayer and carefully instructs her grandchildren in the ways of the church, requiring strict observance of Biblical commandments. When Maya innocently begins a sentence with "by the way," she is punished for taking the Lord's name in vain, because Jesus is "the Way." The incident is illustrative of Momma's profound, even extreme, religious devotion and her determination to inculcate her religious ideals in her grandchildren.

The following document serves as an introduction to the issues considered in this chapter. In his response to some of the criticisms of the African American church, Harry Richardson provides important insight into the weaknesses and strengths of the institution. We then turn to a consideration of the traditional religious testimonies of the African American church, exploring the controversy surrounding the "otherworldliness" of the African American church as well as typical services, the education of preachers, the emotionalism of the services, and the role of music. The concluding section explores the history of Angelou's church, the Christian Methodist Episcopal (C.M.E.) Church, comparing it in terms of its membership, history, and doctrine to other churches frequented by African Americans.

HARRY V. RICHARDSON, FOREWORD TO *DARK GLORY*
(New York: Friendship Press, 1947)

It is generally agreed that the Negro church is the greatest institution developed by Negroes on American soil. It has held in common unity more Negroes than any other organization, and it has had more influence in molding the thought and life of the Negro people than any other single agency. The fact is often overlooked, however, that in its major development and until comparatively recent years, the Negro church was predominantly a rural church. . . .

To be sure, the rural church is and has been open to criticism at many points. For one, its leaders have not always been the men of highest caliber. But when all things are considered, this lack of adequate leadership is more a reflection on education than on the church. Negro theological education, like white education, has in the past made little effort to prepare men for service in the rural field. That is, it has neither trained nor inspired men to serve in an area of great need through an institution that is capable of rendering enormous service.

It has often been said that the rural Negro church has not served as an instrument of protest. In this respect it is compared with other American Negro institutions. The charge that the church has not vigorously or consistently protested against conditions in the South is true. But the charge is often made without seeing the full picture of a lone leader working in the midst of violent, deadly repressive forces, charged with the responsibility of preserving his people who, like himself, are subject to the same destructive pressures. We know now that both the value and effect of a protest are dependent upon the nature of the conscience to which the protest is addressed. The Southern conscience on matters of race today, as in times past, is such as to make unbridled protest questionable, and to make discretion almost imperative in speaking the truth when the larger welfare of the people is involved.

The surplus of emotion, the lack of educated forms, the crude, homely worship of the rural church, are often pointed out in criticism. But again, while valid, the reflection falls elsewhere than on the church. No institution is better than its leaders, and good leaders in large numbers have not been trained to serve the rural church. It has been left in the main to men of lesser gifts, and it reflects all the weaknesses of this desertion. It can be said, too, that not all of the church is unwholesomely emotional, and that much of its emotionality is a hangover from the forms in which Christianity first came to the Negro convert.

When rounded consideration is given to the rural church, it is clear that it stands as the greatest institutional development of Negroes in America. (xi–xiii)

OTHERWORLDLINESS

Like Karl Marx, some have argued that religion has served as the "opiate of the masses," that it has promised eternal reward for the oppressed in the afterlife, and thus has prevented or discouraged meaningful protest and collective resistance to oppression in this life. In the preceding document, Richardson acknowledges the validity of the charge that the African American church has not served as a leader in organizing protest of racial conditions in the South, but he defends the church for its lack of action. In *I Know Why the Caged Bird Sings* Angelou appears to be more critical of the church's failure to concern itself with the here and now. Her lengthy description of a revival meeting emphasizes the other-worldly orientation of the preacher, who takes as the text of his sermon "The least of these," and the contented reaction of the congregation, who believe that "all the Negroes had to do generally, and those at the revival especially, was bear up under this life of toil and cares, because a blessed home awaited them in the far-off bye and bye" (108–9).

Angelou's account suggests that she considers the preacher's message that African Americans should endure and resign themselves to their lot in life to be an inadequate response to their plight. Many scholars have agreed that the African American church has contributed to a lack of militancy among African Americans. E. Franklin Frazier notes in *The Negro Church in America* that "on the whole, the Negro's church was not a threat to white domination and aided the Negro to become accommodated to an inferior status. The religion of the Negro continued to be other-worldly in its outlook, dismissing the privations and sufferings and injustices of this world as temporary and transient" (51). Some scholars have argued that, like violence and segregation, the message of the church has been used to ensure white dominance over blacks. Gary Marx offers an important historical perspective in *Protest and Prejudice*: "Despite occasional controversy over religion's effect, most slave owners eventually came to view supervised religion as an effective means of social control" (95). Marx cites several other sources who make a similar argument for religion's role in maintaining the racial *status quo*, a situation many of these scholars argue continued well into the twentieth century (see Marx, 95, including footnotes).[1] Thus, Angelou's expression of the other-worldly character of the church as recounted in *I Know Why the Caged Bird Sings* is consistent with the views of many who studied the church during the period preceding the civil rights movement. (See also John Dollard's *Caste and Class in a Southern Town* and Benjamin Mays and J. W. Nicholson's *The Negro's Church*.)

The next document offers additional insight into the otherworld-liness of the Church. In Johnson's description of the prayers, ser-mons, and music of a typical Sunday morning service can be seen an emphasis on religion as a comfort in this life and on the need to prepare for the afterlife. In addition, the author, like Harry Rich-ardson, stresses the importance of the institution of the African American church. Finally, Johnson's discussion of the relationship of African American youth to the church in his description of a special Children's Day program has been included here, as it is particularly useful in understanding Angelou's life in the church as a young girl.

CHARLES S. JOHNSON, *GROWING UP IN THE BLACK BELT:
NEGRO YOUTH IN THE RURAL SOUTH*
(Washington, D.C.: American Council on Education, 1941)

Youth and the Church

The Church has been, and continues to be, the outstanding social in-stitution in the Negro community. It has a far wider function than to bring spiritual inspiration to its communicants. Among rural Negroes the church is still the only institution which provides an effective organization of the group, an approved and tolerated place for social activities, a forum for expression on many issues, an outlet for emotional repressions, and a plan for social living. It is a complex institution meeting a wide variety of needs.

In order to understand the behavior of rural Negro youth in relation to the church one must appreciate the cultural aspect of their religion. In the case of the Negro living in the rural South the religious concep-tions and interpretations of doctrine which he expresses have been con-ditioned by his level of culture. Religious attitudes, like other social attitudes, are a part of youth's cultural heritage, and bear the stamp and limitation of the carriers of the culture. The first patterns have come from the parents, and these have been reinforced or redefined by the more formal agencies of religious instruction, the most important of which is the church.

Historically, the formal respect accorded Christianity in America has modified at significant points the expected patterns of treatment for a subject people. Under the slave system, religious gatherings were the first forms of association permitted Negroes, religious teachers were the first leaders allowed to develop, and reading of the Bible was the only tolerated excuse for literacy.

The Negro church came to serve a vital role linked intimately with the status of the race. The doctrine of otherworldliness provided an essential escape from the tedium and tribulations, first of slavery and later of economic serfdom. Educational limitations and the cultural isolation fostered by the rural life of the Negro and by the system of separate social institutions retarded the development of the Negro and stamped him with characteristics associated with the essential patterns of Negro life. Many patterns of religious expression were based upon the practices of white groups not far removed in culture. Frequently, the religious doctrines appropriated were in conflict with pragmatic social values.

The Negro rural church was useful to the older generation of Negroes. The economic homogeneity of the group gave it considerable cohesion. The indifference of the Negro church to current social issues and its emphasis on the values of a future life lent indirect but vital support to the race patterns of the early post-slavery period. The formal ban of the church upon dancing, card playing, and baseball did not seriously trouble the older members because these were not normal expressions of their impulses to recreation and diversion. Other codes of behavior, when in conflict with the folkways of the people, were less conspicuously enforced. The sex mores with which the rural Negro emerged from slavery were a direct result of a situation which prevented an organized family life and the development of personal habits in terms of the standards approved by white society. Through the early period of Negro family organization and the emergence of new values, inconsistencies have appeared between formal codes regarding "illegitimacy," marriage, divorce, and separation, on the one hand, and the requirements for the survival of an "economic family" reinforced by the strength of uncritical custom, on the other. The rural church has been more tolerant of sex mores which violated its codes of conduct than it has of certain forms of recreation such as dancing and card playing.

The introduction by the school of new values stressing literacy, economic improvement, and urbanization has brought significant changes in the role of the rural Negro church in the community. The institution itself has changed but little, but in its function it has a different impact upon new generations of Negroes. In the setting and atmosphere of a typical church and from observation of the character and content of the regular religious instruction, it should be possible to understand more adequately the nature of this impact and the basis for the religious attitudes of rural Negro youth.

A Regular Church Service

Mount Pizgah Church in Johnston County, North Carolina, is a large, gray, single auditorium structure, with high ceiling and long horizontal iron bars overhead to brace the walls. The altar rests at the rear of a small, semicircular platform. There are four chairs directly in front of the platform which are usually occupied by the members of the deacon's board. Back of the altar is a large, frayed, and soiled red plush chair with a high back, in which the minister sits.

The church is filled with perspiring worshippers, both young and old, who are cooling themselves with fans provided by the undertaker. The women are dressed in organdy and voile, and the men in wash pants and shirts. A few wear coats.

After the opening hymn, the congregation is seated; a hard-faced, wiry, dark man remains standing. He is Deacon Eppse, and he prays thus:

> Blessed Jesus, we thank you for life, the greatest blessing in the world, life. We thank you for the blood that circulates through our bodies. We thank you for the blood and the air so we can stand on our feet. We thank you for the loving hand of mercy bestowed upon us; that Thou are in our midst. Prepare us for our souls' journey through this unfriendly world, and when our life on this earth is ended receive us into Thy home which art in heaven.

The congregation sings, "We'll Understand It Better By and By." An elderly brown man of about 65 reads the scripture. There are groans and solemn exclamations from the four men in front of the altar, "Lord have mercy," "Amen." The reader interpolates:

> We have to slip and straighten up the wick in the candle and lamp. We have to straighten up a car. Just like we have to straighten up a wick so the light will burn, and the car so it will run, we have to straighten up our lives so we can go the way our Lord wants us to go.

They sing:

> Almighty God, Almighty God,
> Hold me in the hollow of your hand,
> I'll be your child, I'll be your child,
> Hold me in the hollow of your hand.

The minister comes solemnly forward to the altar. He is a stout and pompous man who continuously rubs a large gold watch chain extended across a prominent waistline.

It's a privilege of mine and a blessing to be here, my friends. Since thirty days ago when we last met many things have been done. Some have gone to their judgment since that time. Gone to meet their Maker and stand in judgment before that stern judge. I'm glad God has spared me to be here. There're some who are sick today who desire this privilege we are enjoying. [Amens] Since we met last, death has reigned right here in our neighborhood. As sure as you see a man living, you see a man who is going to die. You look around you and look at some men and they look like the picture of health. The next thing you know they're dead. That makes us know we got to get on our traveling shoes so we can march right up to our heavenly glory.

You know, I'm a lot old times. I'm one of them that don't go in for new fangled things. And one thing, I got that old time religion, that old time religion that works by faith, that purifies your heart. I ain't got no new religion, and I don't want no new religion. Why, don't you know, with this new religion you can't tell how you got it, and you can't tell where you got it? How you going to tell you got religion at all? I got that same old religion, I can go back to where I got it and tell you all about it. I can tell you how I got it and where I got it any time you ask me. And I can go back to that same old spark and refresh myself and come out stronger in my old time religion. That's what I do all the time—go back to that same old spark. It lighted the way for my father and my mother, and it can light the way for me. [Shouts]

He turns attention to his double text: "If a man die shall he live again," and "I am the resurrection and the life," and discourses at length on the life and trials of Job. The sermon then gets down to everyday experience.

Now I've seen men in critical conditions, sometimes their fingernails decay and come off and disease is destroying their bodies. Sometimes we say sin causes disease. But it's not always so. Sin in the hearts of men causes disease too. I'll make an example. Job was wrapped in sackcloth and ashes a'praying to God, and his wife said, "Look at old Job. He's no good to himself and nobody else. I'm tired of him being sick, and my children's all forsaken me." But Job heard her, and to Almighty God he said, "Lord, though you slay me yet shall I trust you." Job looked at his wife and his wife said, "Curse God and die!" But Job said to her, "Foolish woman, foolish woman.

I brought nothing into the world with me and I'll take nothing out. All the time of my worriation has to be lived out somewhere. [The minister wipes his dripping face, and groans and gasps; the congregation groans and shouts.]

Job took his question to Daniel, and Daniel said, "I saw Him as a stone, hewn out of the mountain." But when Job asked him, "If a man die shall he live again?" Daniel said, "I don't know." Job kept on a'going till he come to Ezekiel, and Ezekiel said, "I saw Him as a wheel within a wheel. I saw Him in the haunts of women." But when Job asked him if a man die shall he rise again, Ezekiel said, "I don't know."

But here comes a man from a new country, a man called Jesus Christ. A man that said, "I am the Son of God, the friend of salvation. I am the lowly fisherman from Galilee. I've seen the face of God. I feed the leprosy cast out by yourself. I can cure the incurable disease. I can perform miracles such as the world has never known." And they brought out the leper, the man dying with that terrible disease, the man everybody shunned and let alone to die. And the Nazarene cured him. [Shouts] Blessed be His name! [Shouts and shrieks]

The congregation is now fully stirred, and its fervent chorus of assent punctuates dramatically the minister's spaced phrases. He refers to the loved ones who have departed, and stresses the certainty of death for everyone.

It don't matter how much you know or how high you climb, you got to die. Mr. Roosevelt, the president of this country's got to die, just like you and I. He can run all these things and do all them big things that everybody talks about, but he's got to lay down and die just the same.

The audience becomes sobered, the preacher lowers his voice:

If we fail to live the life in this world, it'll be too late when we come to cross the River of Jordan. It'll be too late then to get ready. Just like you start dressing at home in your room. You got to get dressed at home before you come out in the street, 'cause if you don't when you get out in the street without no clothes, they'll arrest you and take you to jail. It's too late to get dressed up then. Children, let's dress up and get ready for heaven and glory now. Now's the time to get dressed. Don't wait 'til it's too late. Let's be like Paul was when he said, "I've fought a good fight, I've kept the faith, and now I'm ready for glory."

Another deacon prays. The congregation sings a song about "True Religion" that has many verses, one of which runs:

> Where you going, Elias?
> Where you going, I say?
> Going to the river of Jordan?
> You can't cross there.

They sing of backsliders and cowards. The minister rises in excitement at the close and shouts, "That song is as true as my hand. It's true, true, true. There's not enough words to say it." He then extends an invitation to join the church; no one responds on this occasion. A deacon takes his place behind the collection table.

> Whilst everybody is happy and enjoying this service, we come to you. We know you must have that true religion. But today we want $5.00. We want to get it right at once, quick. Now let everybody push hard while we sing. Let everybody give all he can to the service of the Lord.

The congregation sings a song with verses that could be extended indefinitely:

> It's the walk that you take
> That takes you home.
> It's the prayer that you pray
> That takes you home.

They raise $4.06. After three hours of this worship they go home.

Although the above case study of a Negro church in action during a regular Sunday morning service provides a background for understanding the religious culture in which Negro youth are reared, a still closer view of their relation to the church and of the conflict between the interests of the older and the younger generations in the conduct of the religious services can be had if one visits a special Children's Day program in which the participation of youth is the dominant feature.

A Special Church Service

It is the second Sunday in June and, by tradition, Children's Day at the Piney Grove Baptist Church in Johnston County, North Carolina. This introduces an exciting variation from the routine Sunday services. The whole day can be spent at church. The ten o'clock Sunday school session begins the day, and the regular church service follows around eleven. There will be a heavy basket dinner after the morning service and before the children's program at two o'clock. The young people appear to assume that they have a special privilege of expression on this day, both with respect to the program and the basket dinner. At regular meetings when baskets are brought, the elders have the first round of food at the tables; today there is a protest from the children who want priority rights to the food themselves. As a compromise for Children's Day, special tables are set up so that the young people may eat at the same time as the adults. A few of the liberal adults laugh good humoredly at "the spunk of the youngsters," but the majority of the adults make the concession grudgingly, fearing that one concession may lead to other demands. In many of the churches in the county the Children's Day privilege of eating at the same time as the elders has been flatly refused. The heavy handed domination of the church by the older people and their impatience with the claims of youth for participation are unquestionably responsible for some of the lack of interest on the part of youth in the church.

Children's Day offers a rare opportunity for the youth to parade their talents, in recitations, solos, and management, but there is a fundamental conflict with the deacon's board on the practical value of the occasion. The church needs money and, with all the expenditures for food, there will be little for the church collection. One deacon said, "If they'd put the amount in church they spend for baskets, the church would make some money." They cannot make the children see this, and the conflict increases and may find expression in the church service itself.

Children have come by various methods of conveyance from many sections of the county. They are eager, busy, and excited. The children's program is opened by an awkward youth of 18. He asks, in a shy monotone, if the congregation will sing a selection. Then, one after another, he calls on various youth to appear. They rush to the platform and recite, often in rapid monotone, a poem or a short essay memorized from the *Baptist Guide* (prepared for such occasions) or from various other books of poems. But, shrewdly, the deacons have their way. Between recitations there are competitions among young groups of choristers. As each group sings, a collection is taken, and the audience is urged by the deacons to register their appreciation in the amount of money contributed after each selection. The collection is recorded and contributed to the church in the name of the church or other organizations which the singers represent. After three hours of this program they go home.

Children's Day exercises are held at different churches in the county throughout the month of June. The young people may be observed following the exercises from church to church. Children's Day is their closest approach to self-expression in the church. (135–42)

EMOTIONALISM

An example of emotionalism in the African American church can be seen in the groans, shouts, and shrieks of the congregation in the regular church service described in the preceding document. While Richardson, in *Dark Glory*, blames the lack of training for preachers and the historical origins of the church for this "surplus of emotion" (xiii), Angelou's amusing description of a service at her church suggests that individual members of the congregation can also be catalysts for extreme behavior. She describes Sister Monroe, who, on a particular Sunday, "gets the spirit" and pursues the minister up onto the altar, screaming and grabbing at his clothing (32). Other members of the congregation are similarly inspired, and the incident concludes with the minister, deacon, and chairman of the usher board on the floor following cries, punches, and other physical contact. This incident is a prelude to a second incident on a different Sunday when Sister Monroe assaults a visiting preacher, knocking out his false teeth.

Sister Monroe's emotionalism was not unusual in African American churches. Lincoln and Mamiya cite a visit by W.E.B. Du Bois to a black church, where he observed

the intense enthusiasm and the open display of emotions and feelings exhibited by the worshipers. Some worshipers "got the Spirit" and were propelled into a paroxysm of shouting. While others "fell out" and rolled on the floor in a shaking, trance-like state, possessed by the Holy Ghost. Some people stood up in the pews and waved their hands over their heads, while others clapped their hands in time with the music. Even in the midst of preaching, the worshipers carried on a dialogue with the preacher by shouting approval and agreement with ejaculations like "Amen!" or "Preach it!" or "Tell it like it is!" At other times they encouraged the preacher to work harder to reach that precipitating point of cathartic climax by calling out, "Well?" . . . "Well?" The highlight of the service was to worship and glorify God by achieving the experience of mass catharsis; a purifying explosion of emotions that eclipses the harshness of reality for a season and leaves both the preacher and the congregation drained in a moment of spiritual ecstasy. (5–6)

The next document, from a study of hundreds of African American churches and homes in seventeen counties in the rural South in 1950, explores the training of ministers in this region and gives an account of a West Tennessee revival in order to illustrate some of the techniques used to excite the emotions of the congregation. Once again we can observe the otherworldly emphasis of the text of the sermon preached by the young visiting minister. In addition, the importance of music in the service is quite evident in this description, a phenomenon that will be explored further in the next section of this chapter.

RALPH A. FELTON, *THESE MY BRETHREN: A STUDY OF 570 NEGRO CHURCHES AND 1542 NEGRO HOMES IN THE RURAL SOUTH*
(Madison, N.J.: Drew Theological Seminary, 1950)

The Pastor

Education of the Ministers

The standard training for most American ministers is a four-year college course followed by three years of professional training in a theological seminary. Only 3.9 per cent of the Negro ministers in these 17 counties had received that amount of training.

Fifteen of the 454 ministers, for whom information was available, never attended school in their lives. Nearly half of the pastors (43.3 per cent) have never gotten beyond the eighth grade, and 58.2 per cent have never gone above high school. . . .

In-Service Training

Many of the ministers . . . who had insufficient training when they began to preach are trying to improve themselves. . . . One-third of these men (31.3 percent [of 374 ministers]) are doing little to improve themselves. They have imitated others and developed a pattern of preaching which gets response from their hearers. They believe their hearers need to have their emotions stirred.

"You know, we are an emotional people," is their usual comment on the success of their preaching. Preaching which stirs people's emotions is often called "zooming" or "moaning."

"Man, I sent 'em yesterday!" is the way one minister on Monday morning described his Sunday sermon. He meant he "sent them shouting."

A description of a service in West Tennessee is given here to illustrate some of the methods and techniques used.

Passing several large fine homes with large barns surrounded by mules, tractors and other farm tools, the visitor received a rude jolt in the road which warned him that he was nearing the Browns Creek Baptist Church. This is not an unusual experience for when one enters the Negro Community the roads usually get rougher. One will find less gravel there and sometimes the roads are even impassable.

A group of young people were walking briskly down the road. Pressing the brakes and yelling out "Want a ride?" the driver threw open the door. All accepted and climbed in. We were on our way to Church. We were all relieved when the rear wheels of the automobile cleared the last jagged edge of timber over a small ravine near the church. Just over a little hill loomed the Browns Creek Missionary Baptist Church, brilliantly white against the bright hot August sun. Revivals are always held in August. There was no steeple nor tower to indicate there was a church. However, a crude bell tower stood near the church to call the people to worship. Around the church were scores of automobiles from 1930 models on up. Also there were several wagons with the mules and horses tied to the wheels or to the nearby bushes. A truck or two, also, and a school bus were already parked on the grounds, while hundreds of churchgoers milled about the grounds in Christian fellowship. One of the horses belonged to Deacon Barnes who had left the older son to drive the 1933 Model Ford over with the mother and children, bringing the large box of food—cakes, pies, and chicken which Mrs. Barnes and the girls had prepared Saturday night and Sunday. This was not the only box that was being brought to Browns Creek Church. Scores of others, with a trunk or two thrown in, were also in evidence. A common practice during these August Revivals is "Dinner on the Grounds."

They come from far and near to these Revivals. Really it is a Home-Coming. Inside, the sweet strains of "How Sweet the Sound that Saved a Wretch like Me" were filling the church and overflowing the grounds. People greeted each other in subdued voices as many moved toward the open double door of the rectangular-shaped, low-roofed church.

There were some who never went into the church nor so much as peeped in until attracted by the shouts of happy sisters when the minister was preaching or the quartet was singing.

As the visitor mounted the steps he could feel that they were in need of repair. Caution had to be maintained. Four lady ushers in white uniforms and two male ushers in black pants and white shirts assisted the church goers in locating seats. When a visiting minister arrived he was ushered to the rostrum and seated with some half dozen others who were already sitting there. A hand shake by all the ministers in reach and a kind nod from the rest assured the newcomer he was welcome.

The congregation had reached the last stanza of the hymn "The Lord has promised good to me, his word my hope secures." A motion of the hands by the deacon brought all the congregation except the ministers and a few aged or infirm to their feet, and then a tender request from Deacon Barnes that Brother Jones would lead the prayer brought most of the heads in the church to a lowered position. A few got on their knees. The ministers crossed their legs and tipped their heads on three fingers. The prayer over, the conductor of the prayer service led in singing, "Right Now is a Needy Time." Then he thanked the congregation for participating in the service and turned it over to the pastor. The pastor led in the singing of a few stanzas of "Lord, I want to be a Christian." He expressed pleasure in being alive and present. He expressed expectation of having a great day and a great meeting. He announced that one brother would read the scriptures, another would pray. By this time the choir members had straggled in one by one, to their positions, behind the ministers. When the prayer was completed the choir sang spiritedly. "We are our Heavenly Father's children and we know He loves us one and all." A young visiting minister was persuaded to preach after considerable coaxing by the pastor. His text was "Be Thou Faithful unto the end and I will give thee a Crown of Life." The speaker asked his hearers to be faithful to God and His Church. He pointed out that they could be faithful by coming to the services every day and night this week, by praying and praising God and by giving their means or money to the church. Their reward would be a Crown of Life over yonder in Heaven. The pastor asked that the investigator have some words to say. After he had finished, the pastor then said, "Open the doors of the church for the reception of members." He called for repentance and a new birth. He spoke of the dire fate of those out of the "Ark of Safety." During the singing of "Am I Born to Die, to Lay this Burden Down" people cried out "Amen." Some wept, the minister with the congregation. Two or three of the elderly ladies walked the floor and cried and talked with anyone who would listen, wringing their hands, shaking hands with anyone who was within reach. One young lady who appeared to be about 30 years of age screamed. The pastor looked pleased as the ushers rushed over with fans and ready hands. It was a high moment. The revival service had gotten off to a fine start.

But soon the odor of fried chicken, pies and cakes spread over the church. The pastor said to the Deacons, "We must bring this part of the service to a close."

It is the writer's viewpoint that the emotional phase of worship is the most important of all, but that it is the exploitation of people's emotions in some of these services that is regrettable. (58–61)

MUSIC

In Johnson's descriptions of the church services in *Growing Up in the Black Belt*, in the description of the West Tennessee revival in *These My Brethren*, and in the revival meeting described by Angelou in *I Know Why the Caged Bird Sings*, music plays a prominent role. In *Singin' and Swingin' and Gettin' Merry Like Christmas*, Angelou relates: "When I was growing up in Stamps, Arkansas, Momma used to take me to some church service every day of the week. At each gathering we sang. . . . Our church was bare because the parishioners were poor and our only musical instruments were tambourines and our voices" (74). Religious music sustains Maya's family inside and outside the church. When Momma is taunted by the powhitetrash children (see Chapter 2), she quietly sings several hymns, drawing strength from the music in much the same way that slaves were comforted by spirituals.

Historically, music has been an important feature of the religious expression of African Americans. In their first preface to *The Books of American Negro Spirituals*, James Weldon Johnson and J. Rosamond Johnson explain that the spirituals originated with the slaves and that, like the sermons discussed earlier in this chapter, the focus was otherworldly:

> Far from his native land and customs, despised by those among whom he lived, experiencing the pang of the separation of loved ones on the auction block, knowing the hard task master, feeling the lash, the Negro seized Christianity, the religion of compensations in the life to come for the ills suffered in the present existence, the religion which implied the hope that in the next world there would be a reversal of conditions, of rich man and poor man, of proud and meek, of master and slave. The result was a body of songs voicing all the cardinal virtues of Christianity—patience—forbearance—love—faith—and hope—through a necessarily modified form of African music. The Negro took complete refuge in Christianity, and the Spirituals were literally forged of sorrow in the heat of religious fervor. (20)

In his analysis of what he calls "the Sorrow Songs" of the slaves in *The Souls of Black Folk*, W.E.B. Du Bois further elaborates the themes of the spirituals:

Through all the sorrow of the Sorrow Songs there breathes a hope—a faith in the ultimate justice of things. The minor cadences of despair change often to triumph and calm confidence. Sometimes it is faith in life, sometimes a faith in death, sometimes assurance of boundless justice in some fair world beyond. But whichever it is, the meaning is always clear: that sometime, somewhere, men will judge men by their souls and not by their skins. (189)

Angelou notes the common themes present in the songs sung at the revival and the blues heard on the way home: "A stranger to the music could not have made a distinction between the songs sung a few minutes before and those being danced to in the gay house by the railroad tracks. All asked the same questions. How long, oh God? How long?" (111).

The next document contains material from the introduction and conclusion to James H. Cone's *The Spirituals and the Blues: An Interpretation*. Cone, like Angelou, grew up in a small African American community in Arkansas and, like Angelou, he notes the similarities between the themes and purposes of the spirituals and the blues. These two musical expressions of African Americans may seem quite different on the surface, but according to both Angelou and Cone, they share a profound connection. Each in its own way expresses the yearnings of African Americans and their determination to endure.

JAMES H. CONE, *THE SPIRITUALS AND THE BLUES: AN INTERPRETATION* (1972)
(Reprint. Maryknoll, N.Y.: Orbis Books, 1991)

The power of song in the struggle for black survival—that is what the spirituals and blues are about. I grew up in a small black community in Bearden, Arkansas, where black music was essential for identity and survival. On Saturday nights the juke box was loud, and one could hear the sound and feel the rhythm of the blues even from a distance. The men and women gathered around the juke box had worked long hours during the week in saw mills and factories; by Saturday night they were tired and weary. They needed to express their moods and feelings, their joys and sorrows. They needed to refresh their spirits in the sound and rhythm of black humanity. And they did, sometimes peaceably and sometimes violently, often doing to each other what they wished they could do to white people. But chiefly they enjoyed themselves. Little Milton was always a favorite. . . .

But not every black in Bearden responded spontaneously to Little Milton and his interpretation of the blues. These latter preferred the other musical expression of black people, called "church music" or the spirituals, and Sunday was their time to unleash the pent-up emotions of their being. At Macedonia A.M.E. Church, the Spirit of God was no abstract concept, no vague perception of philosophical speculation. The Spirit was the "power of God unto salvation," that "wheel in the middle of the wheel." The Spirit was God breaking into the lives of the people, "buildin' them up where they were torn down and proppin' them up on every leanin' side." The Spirit was God's presence with the people and God's will to provide them the courage and the strength to make it through. And the people were thankful for God's presence and renewed weekly their covenant to "hold out to the end." . . .

At Macedonia A.M.E. Church the melody, rhythm, and style were black; the mood was black; and the people were black. Everything they did was a valiant attempt to define and structure the meaning of blackness—so that their children and their children's children would be a little "freer" than they were. They had a "hard row to hoe" and a "rocky road to travel," and they had made it and intended to make it "through the storm." (1–2)

Whatever form black music takes, it is always an expression of black life in America and what the people must do to survive with a measure of dignity in a society which seems bent on destroying their right to be human beings. The fact that black people keep making music means that we as a people refuse to be destroyed. We refuse to allow the people who oppress us to have the last word about our humanity. The last word belongs to us and music is our way of saying it. Contrary to popular opinion, therefore, the spirituals and the blues are not songs of despair or of a defeated people. On the contrary, they are songs which represent one of the great triumphs of the human spirit. (130)

HISTORY OF THE C.M.E. CHURCH

The remainder of this chapter explores the history of the denomination to which Angelou belongs, the Christian Methodist Episcopal Church. It considers the origins of the church, how its early beginnings contributed to the otherworldly focus noted by Angelou, its membership, and how the C.M.E. Church compares to other churches attended by African Americans in terms of membership, origins, and philosophy.

Religious Bodies: 1936, published by the Bureau of the Census, provides a historical account of the place of African Americans in the church, first as slaves under the auspices of the Methodist Church in the South, and later as the independent Colored Methodist Episcopal Church (renamed the Christian Methodist Episcopal Church in 1954). In addition, the document provides some insight into the theological doctrine of the church. It is interesting that this presumably objective account gives no hint of the controversy surrounding the origins of the C.M.E. Church (see "Other Accounts of the Origins of the C.M.E. Church" for a discussion of this controversy).

U.S. DEPARTMENT OF COMMERCE, BUREAU OF THE CENSUS,
RELIGIOUS BODIES: 1936, VOLUME 2, PART 2
(Washington, D.C.: GPO, 1941)

Denominational History

The history of Negroes as an integral and inseparable element of the Methodist Church in the South dates from the earliest appearance of the Methodist Church in that section. From the very beginning, the promoters of the Methodist Church showed interest in the slaves and accordingly evangelistic campaigns were conducted among the slaves who then were very numerous on the large and small southern plantations. Even prior to the break between the northern and southern wings of the then united Methodist Church, in 1844, the Methodist Church had so-called "mixed" congregations composed of white and Negro members.

There were instances when and where the two races—one the landowners and the other Negro slaves—used the same churches for both races for worship. In some cases different hours were used, while in still rarer instances white people and Negro slaves met in the same building at the same time, certain places being assigned slaves. The slaves in some sections had their own small and unpretentious churches, where occasionally a white minister of the Methodist Church did the preaching and exhorting.

In a few instances Negroes who showed sufficient aptitude, talent, intelligence, and effectiveness were permitted to exhort and preach to the people of their own race. This was permitted, however, only under supervision of the plantation owner.

It might be cited for illustration that several of the Southern States of the slaveholding area took drastic actions to restrict the religious freedom of the Negro slaves following the insurrection movements for freedom on the part of such historic Negro leaders as Denmark Vesey, Gabriel Prosser, and Nat Turner near the middle of the nineteenth century.

Particularly did the South react to restrain and restrict the Negro's religious freedom following the Nat Turner insurrection. Southern plantation owners were particularly incensed against Negro preachers, and legal measures were enacted in the Southern States making it a serious offense for Negro preachers to minister to the religious and spiritual needs of Negroes in the absence of white people. . . .

Reference has already been made to the split within the Methodist Church, North and South, which came over the slave issue in 1844–45.

The southern delegates of the Methodist Church resented the effort to discipline Bishop James O. Andrew, who was charged with "holding slaves." Accordingly they withdrew and formed a church of their own and took the name of the Methodist Episcopal Church, South.

Because of the deep feeling of resentment on the part of the southern white plantation owners toward Negro ministers, and since white ministers for a time were not over much enamored with the idea of improving the Negro's status, there were years of religious neglect and abandonment almost in its entirety. This could be termed the period of religious forgetfulness of the Negro, as the South broadcast the rumor that Nat Turner was a preacher. Thus, Negro preachers in all the Southern States wore the stigma of "using preaching as a means to incite their race to servile insurrection."

When the division over the slave issue came in 1844, the Methodist Episcopal Church, South, naturally had a huge following in its membership among the slaves. Estimate on a conservative scale claims there were 158,000 Negro slaves members of the Southern Methodist Church. Within the short span of 15 years, 1860, by the same conservative estimate, the Methodist Episcopal Church, South, had a slave membership of between 225,000 and 250,000.

With the Emancipation Proclamation, the Civil War, the Reconstruction period and the general devastating demoralization which followed, all of the slave membership of the Southern Methodist Episcopal Church, except approximately 80,000, joined the two independent Negro Methodist bodies which had seceded from the Methodist Church, while a few cast their lot with the northern branch of the Methodist Church, which welcomed them into its Negro congregations which sprang up in various sections of the South almost overnight.

On this matter, the words of the late Bishop Robert Williams, for 40 years a powerful figure in the Colored Methodist Episcopal Church, are very comprehensive, concise, pertinent, and pointed. He wrote:

The Emancipation Proclamation produced at once a crisis in the affairs of the colored church members. Before the war, so far as the Methodist churches were concerned, the slaves worshiped with their owners, the gallery or some other section of the building being set apart for them. If a special "meetinghouse" was provided, the colored congregation was treated as an appendage to the white, being served once a month, usually on the Sabbath afternoon, or if in cities, every Sabbath afternoon; separate official meetings were held, also, and separate financial and statistical reports were made at the annual conference.

Under the new order this method of ministering to the growing needs of the colored members grew very unsatisfactory to them and they sent a special commission to meet with the mother church in General Conference assembled in New Orleans in 1866, this commission to represent their expressed needs and desires for separation and organization into a distinct colored church of their own. A committee was appointed to consider the religious interests of the colored people and submitted two reports, one of which was as follows:

Your committee recommends the adoption of the following in reference to the education of the colored people:

Whereas the condition of the colored people of the South is now essentially changed; and

Whereas the interests of the white and colored people are materially dependent upon the intelligence and virtue of this race, that we have had and must continue to have among us; and

Whereas the Methodist Episcopal Church, South, has always claimed to be the friend of that people, a claim vindicated by the conscious and successful exertions made in their behalf, in instructing and evangelizing them; and it is important that we continue to evince our interest for them in this regard; and as our hearts prompt us to this philanthropy; therefore, be it

Resolved, That we recommend to our people the establishment of day schools, under proper regulations and trustworthy teachers, for the education of colored children.

The other report presented the following answers to the question, "What shall be done to promote the religious interest of colored people?"

1. Let our colored members be organized as separate pastoral charges, wherever they prefer it, and their numbers justify it.

2. Let each pastoral charge of colored members have its own quarterly conference composed of official members, as provided for in the discipline.

3. Let colored persons be licensed to preach, and ordained deacons and elders, according to the discipline, where in the judgment of the conference having jurisdiction in the case, they are deemed suitable persons for said office and order in the ministry. . . .

Thus, it is obvious that the Colored Methodist Episcopal Church is the legitimate offspring of regular Methodist stock; that it originated not out of schism and secession but was rather set-up and apart as a distinct Methodist body by mutual agreement between the Negro and white membership of the Methodist Episcopal Church, South.

Through the intervening years the members of the Colored Methodist Episcopal Church have maintained a very intimate, unique, and helpful relationship to the Southern Methodist Episcopal Church to which the constituency of the Colored Methodist Episcopal Church affectionately refers as "the mother church." On the other hand the Southern Methodist Episcopal Church has welcomed the appellation and from time to time has made substantial missionary and educational contributions to the schools and churches of the Colored Methodist Episcopal Church.

Doctrine

The Colored Methodist Episcopal Church is in complete harmony with the Methodist Episcopal Church. In theology the Colored Methodist Episcopal Church is strictly Arminian and its doctrinal tenets are specifically set forth in the Article of Religion and the New Testament. In the body of doctrines is that of the Holy Trinity; virgin birth; man's fall; necessity for repentance and restitution from sin; the freedom of the will; sanctification; punishment for unrighteous living and just rewards for righteous living; and the all sufficiency of the Scriptures for human salvation. . . .

The sole condition which is a prerequisite for admission to membership in the Colored Methodist Episcopal Church is "a desire to flee from the wrath to come and to be saved from their sins." . . . (1217–20).

OTHER ACCOUNTS OF THE ORIGINS OF THE C.M.E. CHURCH

In *The Rise of "Colored Methodism,"* Othal Hawthorne Lakey points out several unique aspects that distinguish the C.M.E. Church from other African American churches:

> It is the only independent Negro Methodist body organized in full cooperation with, and the ecclesiastical and legal authority of, the white denomination from which separation took place. It is the only Negro Church strictly Southern in its initial organization consisting almost if not entirely of ex-slaves in which no Negroes free prior to the Civil War played any role. It is the only one which sought co-operation and assistance from *Southern* whites, but rejected Northern white (and black) political alliances and religious influence. (3–4)

The Circuit Rider Dismounts: A Social History of Southern Methodism, 1865–1900 by Hunter Dickinson Farish shows that there was some controversy involved in the founding of the C.M.E. Church that the Bureau of the Census document and Lakey's account do not mention.

> The Colored Methodist Episcopal Church, because of its friendliness to its parent Church, was declared to be a fit place for only such as desired to be in slavery. It was derided as "the Rebel Church," the "Democratic Church," the "old slavery Church," and "the kitchen Church." The spirit manifested toward the Methodist Episcopal Church, South, and the Colored Methodist Episcopal Church is reflected in a comment made by the Atlanta *Methodist Advocate* in 1871. Referring to the organization of the colored Conferences of the Southern body into an independent General Conference, it said: "They are evidently out of the church, South, and we congratulate them on getting out, though by the back door, through the kitchen." (173)

Lincoln and Mamiya report that the C.M.E. Church was restricted from engaging in any type of political activity upon its separation from the Methodist Episcopal Church, South. Thus, "because the

C.M.E. Church began under such strictures and because it lacked the tradition of the African societies and abolitionist involvement, its early development bore the stigma of ultraconservatism and political inconsequence" (62).

Finally, James A. Anderson's account of the founding of the C.M.E. Church in *Centennial History of Arkansas Methodism* provides insight into the paternalism and self-interest of white Southern Methodists in agreeing to have separate Methodist churches for blacks and whites:

Always up to the war we had considerable Negro membership, which we included in our figures, though written separately in the tables. There were in the Southern Methodist Church when the war closed something over 200,000 Negro members, won from their African superstitions. It was a remarkable missionary achievement, one of the most significant in Church history. But as soon as the war was over the carpetbaggers had a gospel to preach to the Negroes. We soon saw that they were destined to lead them all away from us, and, to protect them by keeping them out of the hands of such missionaries, we set them up into a Church of their own, ordaining bishops for them, the name of this church being, as at this hour, "The Colored Methodist Episcopal Church." This action was not taken, however, till 1870, and by that time we could muster only fifty or sixty thousand of them. *But they have been and are among the best Negroes in the world, keeping freer from "politics" and other foolishness than any other Negroes in this country* [emphasis added]. We are yet fostering their schools, such as Paine College in Georgia and Haygood Institute in Arkansas, though we have never done as much for them as they deserve. (101)

In regard to membership, it has already been noted in the excerpt from the Bureau of the Census publication *Religious Bodies: 1936* that many African Americans left the Methodist Church, South before the founding of the C.M.E. Church for two other independent African American Methodist bodies: the African Methodist Episcopal (A.M.E.) Church and the African Methodist Episcopal Zion (A.M.E.Z.) Church. Lakey explains the differences between the "Colored Methodism" of the C.M.E. Church and the "African Methodism" of the A.M.E. Church and the A.M.E.Z. Church, stemming from their different origins:

"Colored Methodism" recognized that plantation slavery rendered the newly freed Negro culturally unequal to the Southern whites and thus unable to participate on an equal basis with the whites in the *total* social process. Subsequently, for Colored Methodism a religion unencumbered by partisan political activity, but supported by cordial relations with Southern whites was essential to lifting the cultural level of the Negro, thus *preparing* him for political and social equality. "African Methodism" on the other hand viewed the freed Negro in terms of his African cultural heritage and therefore considered the Negro ready for full social and political [e]quality. Consequently, for African Methodism, a significant part of religion among Negroes was fostering full political involvement and social equality. (5)

We will conclude with a comparison of the growth in membership for all three African American Methodist churches from 1856 to 1972 taken from Harry V. Richardson's *Dark Salvation* (253). The table shows that membership in the C.M.E. Church has grown steadily since 1880, but that its membership still lags behind the other two African American Methodist churches.

Denomination	1856	1880	1906	1926	1972
A.M.E.	19,963	400,000	600,000	750,000	1,100,000
A.M.E.Z.	4,600	250,000	350,000	500,000	770,000
C.M.E.		120,000	250,000	350,000	466,000

NOTE

1. It should be noted that not all scholars agree that the church has served only conservative interests. In particular, its role in the civil rights movement raises questions about the African American church's reactionary reputation. Gary Marx points out that "it was in the church that many leaders were exposed to a broad range of ideas legitimizing protest and obtained the *savoir faire*, self-confidence, and organizational experience needed to challenge an oppressive system" (96). Marx mentions Martin Luther King among others in support of this view and undertakes to answer the question "Religion: Opiate or Inspiration of Civil Rights Militance?" in chapter 4 of his work. Marx's conclusions were challenged by Larry and Janet Hunt; the title of their article is indicative of their conclusions: "Black Religion as *Both* Opiate and Inspiration of Civil Rights Militance: Putting Marx's Data to the Test." Lincoln and Mamiya suggest

that there is a dialectic between the otherworldly and this-worldly ori-
entations. They write: "Past studies have overemphasized the other-
worldly views of black churches. The other-worldly aspect, the
transcendence of social and political conditions, can have a this-worldly
political correlate which returns to this world by providing an ethical and
prophetic critique of the present social order" (12).

STUDY QUESTIONS

1. Historically, when and under what circumstances were African Americans introduced to Christianity?

2. According to the documents in this chapter, what positive contributions has the African American church made to the African American community?

3. What are some of the criticisms that have been leveled at the African American church?

4. What are some of the themes expressed in the prayers and sermons in the regular church service described by Johnson in *Growing Up in the Black Belt*?

5. Based on Johnson's account, what is the role of children in the church?

6. According to Lincoln and Mamiya, Felton and others, why is emotionalism a significant aspect of some African American religious services?

7. What is the role of music in African American churches?

8. What are some of the themes associated with African American religious music?

9. Discuss the circumstances surrounding the founding of the Christian Methodist Episcopal Church.

10. In what ways is the history of the C.M.E. Church different from that of the other two black Methodist churches, the African Methodist Episcopal (A.M.E.) Church and the African Methodist Episcopal Zion (A.M.E.Z) Church?

TOPICS FOR WRITTEN OR ORAL EXPLORATION

1. Taking into consideration the writings of scholars who emphasize the otherworldly orientation of the African American church as well as those of scholars with alternative perspectives, what is your opinion regarding the positive or negative impact on the African American community of the African American Church?

2. From your reading of the various episodes touching on religion in *I Know Why the Caged Bird Sings*, including the complete description of the revival meeting, what is your interpretation of Angelou's attitude toward her religious environment?

3. How do the descriptions of the church services in Johnson's *Growing*

Up in the Black Belt and the West Tennessee revival meeting in Felton's *These My Brethren* compare to Angelou's descriptions of religious services in *I Know Why the Caged Bird Sings*? What similarities and differences do you see in these accounts?

4. According to James Cone, what similarities exist between the spirituals and the blues? From your knowledge of contemporary African American music, including rap music, do these similarities exist in popular African American music today?

5. Taking into consideration the various accounts of the founding of the C.M.E. Church, why have some analysts been critical of the C.M.E. Church's historical role in social and political movements?

WORKS CITED

Anderson, James A. *Centennial History of Arkansas Methodism: A History of the Methodist Episcopal Church, South, in the State of Arkansas 1815–1935*. Benton, Ark.: L. B. White Printing Co., 1935.

Angelou, Maya. *I Know Why the Caged Bird Sings*. 1970. Toronto: Bantam Books, 1971.

———. *Singin' and Swingin' and Gettin' Merry Like Christmas*. 1976. Toronto: Bantam Books, 1977.

Dollard, John. *Caste and Class in a Southern Town*. New York: Oxford University Press, 1938.

Du Bois, W.E.B. *The Souls of Black Folk*. 1953. Greenwich, Conn.: Fawcett, 1961, 1968.

Farish, Hunter Dickinson. *The Circuit Rider Dismounts: A Social History of Southern Methodism, 1865–1900*. Richmond, Va.: Dietz Press, 1938.

Frazier, E. Franklin. *The Negro Church in America*. 1964. New York: Schocken Books, 1974.

Hunt, Larry L., and Janet G. Hunt. "Black Religion as *Both* Opiate and Inspiration of Civil Rights Militance: Putting Marx's Data to the Test." *Social Forces* 56, 1 (September 1977): 1–14.

Johnson, James Weldon, and J. Rosamond Johnson. *The Books of American Negro Spirituals*. New York: Viking Press, 1925.

Lakey, Othal Hawthorne. *The Rise of "Colored Methodism": A Study of the Background and the Beginnings of the Christian Methodist Episcopal Church*. Dallas: Crescendo Book Publications, 1972.

Lincoln, C. Eric, and Lawrence H. Mamiya. *The Black Church in the African American Experience*. Durham: Duke University Press, 1990.

Marx, Gary. *Protest and Prejudice: A Study of Belief in the Black Community*. New York: Harper and Row, 1967.

Mays, Benjamin, and Joseph Nicholson. *The Negro's Church*. New York: Institute of Social and Religious Research, 1933.

Richardson, Harry V. *Dark Salvation: The Story of Methodism as It Developed Among Blacks in America*. Garden City, N.Y.: Anchor Press/Doubleday, 1976.

SUGGESTED READINGS

See the full text of works excerpted in this chapter.

Christopher, Stefan C. "The Negro Church in the U.S.A." *Organon* 2 (1971): 4–12.

Johnson, Joseph A. *Basic Christian Methodist Beliefs*. Memphis: CME Church Publishing, 1978.

Lakey, Othal Hawthorne. *The History of the CME Church*. Memphis: CME Publishing House, 1985.

Phillips, C. H. *The History of the Colored Methodist Episcopal Church in America*. New York: Arno Press, 1972.

Roberts, Harry W. "The Rural Negro Minister: His Personal and Social Characteristics." *Social Forces* 27 (March 1949): 291–300.

Thurman, Howard. *The Negro Spiritual Speaks of Life and Death*. New York: Harper and Row, 1947.

Turner, Ronny E. "The Black Minister: Uncle Tom or Abolitionist?" *Phylon* 34 (1960): 86–95.

Washington, Joseph R., Jr. *Black Religion: The Negro and Christianity in the U.S.* Boston: Beacon, 1964.

Woodson, Carter. *The History of the Negro Church*. Washington, D.C.: Associated Publishers, 1921.

5

The African American Family and Other Role Models

THE GRANDMOTHER, MOTHER, AND MATRIARCHY

The importance of family and of other influential people in Maya Angelou's journey toward self-acceptance and independence cannot be overstated. From her neighbor Mrs. Flowers's healing intervention after Maya is raped to her brother Bailey's unconditional love, Maya is fortunate to have the love and support of those around her. Angelou notes the significant role played by extended family and friends in her upbringing. Pointing out that she was raised by her grandmother and her Uncle Willie up to the age of thirteen, she adds: "But the people around us also helped raise us. They watched us when we were out of the house. They knew that Mamma was getting up in age and Uncle Willie could not get around easily, so they watched us and reported our actions to Mamma and Uncle Willie" (Angelou, Interview with Randall-Tsuruta, 4–5).

Perhaps no one had greater influence on Maya's early development than Momma, Angelou's grandmother, with whom Maya and Bailey were sent to live after their parents' divorce. Although Annie Henderson is not openly affectionate with her grandchildren, it is clear that Maya feels deeply loved by her grandmother.

The way Annie Henderson takes responsibility for her extended family is consistent with E. Franklin Frazier's analysis of the importance of grandmothers in the African American family. In a chapter entitled "Granny: The Guardian of the Generations" in *The Negro Family in the United States*, Frazier provides a historical perspective for this phenomenon:

> During slavery the Negro grandmother occupied in many instances an important place in the plantation economy and was highly esteemed by both the slaves and the masters. . . . She was the repository of the accumulated lore and superstition of the slaves and was on hand at the birth of black children as well as white. She took under her care the orphaned and abandoned children. . . . When emancipation came, it was often the old grandmother who kept the generations together. (114–16)

Frazier cites a former slave who has assumed the care of her relatives: "Me being the oldest one and me being they mother's auntie and the oldest head, that's how I come by them" (117). Frazier explains: "This old woman expresses the characteristic attitude of the grandmother in her role as 'oldest head' in the family. Where the maternal family organization assumes such importance as among a large section of the Negro population, the oldest woman is regarded as the head of the family" (117).

While some analysts have viewed the importance of grandmothers and other extended family members as a sign of disorganization and pathology (the next document is a case in point), others have countered that the role of the extended family is a unique strength of the African American family. In their recent study of Holmes County, Mississippi entitled "The Black Extended Family: A Basic Rural Institution and a Mechanism of Urban Adaptation," Shimkin et al. write:

> Both sexes feel an obligation to provide babies with physical affection, while contingent responsibility for the protection, care, instruction, and discipline of all children is diffused among related adults and, indeed, all adults. Whether the relationships are actually centered in the biological family depends upon circumstances and personalities. Children are readily transferred from the care of an unmarried mother or immature parents, say, to that of grandparents or an uncle and aunt. Less crowding in one household than in another, the availability of Head Start, or better schooling may moti-

vate such adaptive shifts. These are designed for the children's welfare and may, in fact, be initiated by them. Often characterizing the behavior of strong and cohesive extended families, such foster-ages are not abandonments of parental responsibility but rather sharings in the deep satisfaction felt by Holmes Countians in child rearing. (72)

In her much earlier 1939 study of the Deep South, Hortense Powdermaker also takes a positive view of what she calls the "elasticity" of African American families, which are more likely than white families to include members outside the nuclear family:

> In most Negro households, grandparents, nieces, nephews, adopted children, and others who are not related even by adoption, commonly form part of the family group; and members of the real family are as commonly absent. . . . It is by now a well-established generalization that the typical Negro family throughout the South is matriarchal and elastic, in striking contrast to the more rigid and patriarchal family organization of occidental white culture. (143)

But despite the positive aspects of finding a home with extended family members, it should be noted that both Maya and Bailey suffer from their parents' absence. They blame themselves for their parents' divorce and separation from them. When they are reunited with their mother during a yearlong stay in St. Louis, Maya is ever-conscious of the fact that she cannot depend on her and fears that she could be sent back to Stamps at any time. In a 1983 interview, Angelou commented that Vivian Baxter "was a poor mother for a child" (Interview with Paterson, 422). Nevertheless, in another interview, Angelou indicated that although she only lived with her mother intermittently and for short periods until she was thirteen, her mother has been a powerful role model for her: "I'm often asked how I got over that without holding a grudge. I see her as one of the greatest human beings I've ever met" (Interview with Oliver, 114).

Vivian Baxter's influence is most clearly seen during the period Maya is living with her in California. When Maya decides to become the first black streetcar conductorette, her mother initially warns her that African Americans are not hired for this work. But once she sees Maya's determination to challenge this discriminatory situation, she gives her unflagging support.

In *Singin' and Swingin' and Gettin' Merry Like Christmas* Angelou credits both her mother's and her grandmother's example for her refusal to go on welfare while struggling to raise her son Guy as a single mother:

> My pride had been starched by a family who assumed unlimited authority in its own affairs. A grandmother, who raised me, my brother and her own two sons, owned a general merchandise store. She had begun her business in the early 1900's in Stamps, Arkansas, by selling meat pies to saw men in a lumber mill, then racing across town in time to feed workers in a cotton-gin mill four miles away. . . . My beautiful mother, who ran businesses and men with autocratic power, taught me to row my own boat, and paddle my own canoe, hoist my own sail. She warned, in fact, "If you want something done, do it yourself." (10–11)

There is no doubt that Vivian Baxter practices what she preaches. In California she initially provides the economic support for her children. When Maya and Bailey want to know what she does for a living, she describes her work in the saloons and gambling dens with characteristic honesty. Later, Vivian Baxter marries Daddy Clidell, and the family's financial situation is further secured by Clidell's real estate holdings and the series of roomers who share their fourteen-room house in San Francisco. (By the end of the second volume of Angelou's autobiography, Vivian and Daddy Clidell are divorced [*Gather Together in My Name*, 170].)

Despite her occasional economic dependence on male lovers or husbands (in St. Louis her boyfriend, Mr. Freeman, provides the basic necessities), Vivian Baxter never appears to be controlled by the men in her life, nor will she allow her daughter to be. When she learns that Maya is pregnant, she asks if Maya loves the father and if he loves her. When the answer to both questions is no, she matter-of-factly accepts that her daughter will be an unwed mother. In the course of *I Know Why the Caged Bird Sings*, Maya's mother, already divorced from Bailey Johnson, Sr., lives with Mr. Freeman (who is promptly arrested after raping Maya), and finally marries Daddy Clidell, whom Angelou suggests she was initially prepared to dismiss as just one more of her mother's lovers.

The next document demonstrates that Vivian Baxter's ability to provide for herself, her sexual independence, and her dominant role in her family can be understood in light of historical antecedents. It highlights the role of the mother during slavery and after Emancipation and provides a historical context for the matriarchal structure of many African American families. Finally, it helps explain why, in Angelou's account of her family life, her grandmother and mother are such prominent figures, while her father appears as a more marginal character.

ABRAM KARDINER AND LIONEL OVESEY, *THE MARK OF OPPRESSION: EXPLORATIONS IN THE PERSONALITY OF THE AMERICAN NEGRO* (1951)
(Reprint. Cleveland: Meridian, 1962)

During slavery the Negro family was an approximation of the white pattern. It was aided by white masters. This was for purposes of intra-plantation stability. In some plantations three-generation families were kept intact. These were temporary arrangements which were not institutionalized, but, at the time, happened to be best suited to the interests of the landowner.

Under these conditions, the mother-child tie had to be respected and the female became the emotional center of the family. When a male slave was sold, he went alone; when a female slave was sold, the children generally went with her, unless they were sufficiently grown to become independent pieces of property. The mother became the central figure and the prime authority. . . . This condition was fixed still more by the common practice of the whites, who used the female slaves as concubines. Whether free or slave, the Negro female had many advantages in permitting intimacies with white men. In other words, the Negro female broke the caste system and entered upon a limited emotional reciprocity with her white master. But no matter what variants were introduced into this situation, the Negro mother remained the center of her household, and the father, white or black, was distinctly in the background.

The situation with the "free" Negroes was about the same. Marriages were definitely less stable than in whites [*sic*], and promiscuity was the rule. The female under these conditions retained her dominant position in the household. The stability of the Negro family and its resemblance to the white pattern increased according to the economic stability of the Negro male. Hence, the female-centered family is most characteristic of the South. This has one prominent variant in the form of the grandmother-centered family. Migration of males to the North was one of the strong contributors to the uterine family. In the North, the largest number of families with female heads is to be found in the lowest classes, i.e., those that are the worse off economically. This is the ultimate consequence of the higher economic value of the female and the greater relative economic insecurity of the male. During slavery, the female took the dominant role by virtue of her higher sexual value. After emancipation she retained this dominance, but this time through her greater economic value.

The Negro family, particularly in the lower classes, suffers a great deal of disorganization. Basic here is the lesser economic opportunity of the Negro male. His inability to meet familial obligations finds its ultimate expression in the large number of broken homes among Negroes, as well as in the large number of families with female heads. In the United States in 1940, broken families were 28 per cent of all Negro families, but only 12 per cent of white families. Likewise, the percentage of Negro families with female heads in cities with a total population of 100,000 or over ranged from 21 to 34. These figures reflect not only a higher separation and divorce rate for Negroes, but also a higher desertion rate for Negro males, since the large number of homes with female heads is not accounted for solely by widowhood, divorce, and legal separation.

The economic necessity for sharing households—"doubling up"—is another factor that contributes to Negro family disorganization. Many more Negro families have grandchildren living with them than do white families. More Negro households have relatives other than parents, grandparents, and children. . . . Lodgers and "one person" families constituted 10 per cent of the total Negro population in 1940, whereas the corresponding figure for the white population was 5 per cent.

These facts must be contrasted with the basic patriarchal orientation of the white family. A new source of difficulty in the Negro household is introduced by the tradition of expectancy of male dominance. In other words, a Negro female loses respect for her spouse whose economic condition prevents him from acting according to white ideals or prototypes. The unhappy economic plight of the Negro male not only contributes to the economic dominance of the Negro female, but also makes her psychologically dominant. Such a situation does not enhance family cohesion. It also renders the female less likely to make the effort to hold her husband or to try to get him back, once he is gone.

Perhaps the best index of family stability that is available is that of illegitimacy. For the United States as a whole in 1944 Negroes (non-whites) had about eight and a half times as much illegitimacy as whites.

[The authors indicate in a footnote that they have drawn freely from E. Franklin Frazier's *The Negro Family in the United States* (University of Chicago Press, 1939) for this analysis.]

ROLE MODELS

Maya Angelou has cited numerous role models for her life and work, and for African Americans in general. In an interview with Claudia Tate, she asserted that whites and males are dominant in the world and that they must be countered with other role models, from family members to historical heroines:

> We need to see our mothers, aunts, our sisters, and grandmothers. We need to see Frances Harper, Sojourner Truth, Fannie Lou Hammer, women of our heritage. We need to have these women preserved. We need them all: . . . Constance Motley, Etta Motten. . . . All of these women are important as role models. Depending on our profession, some may be even more important. Zora Neale Hurston means a great deal to me as a writer. (2)

When asked in the same interview about other writers who have influenced her work, Angelou mentioned several—James Baldwin, Toni Morrison, Rosa Guy, Ann Petry, Joan Didion—but she acknowledged as particularly important "two men who probably formed my writing ambition more than any others. They were Paul La[u]rence Dunbar and William Shakespeare" (11).

In *I Know Why the Caged Bird Sings* Angelou gives special recognition to the importance of black poets. After the disastrous speech by the white speaker at her graduation, Maya and her classmates are saved from self-hatred by the class valedictorian, who leads the audience in singing "Lift Ev'ry Voice and Sing" by James Weldon Johnson and J. Rosamond Johnson.

In another episode with striking similarities to the highs and lows of her eighth-grade graduation, Angelou remembers the significance of the boxer Joe Louis for African Americans. She describes the crowding of men, women, and children into her grandmother's general store to listen to a radio broadcast of Louis's fight with Primo Carnera. From Angelou's description it appears that the outcome of the fight has a direct correlation to her people's destiny and self-worth. When Louis is declared the winner, she exults: "Joe Louis had proved that we were the strongest people in the world" (115).

The pride Joe Louis inspired in African Americans is further seen in this quote from a 1940 biographical entry in *Current Biography*: "He is the idol of every Negro home in the United States. In Harlem hundreds of Negro children, cats and dogs are named after him" (524). The day after Louis's fight with Carnera, the *New York Times* featured the following article describing the celebration of thousands of African Americans in Harlem. The article confirms Angelou's perspective on the significance of the fight for African Americans.

"THOUSANDS IN HARLEM CELEBRATE LOUIS VICTORY"
(*New York Times*, June 26, 1935, 24)

Harlem outdid New Year's Eve last night in its celebration of Joe Louis's fistic victory over Primo Carnera. Between 125th and 145th Streets, along Lenox and Seventh Avenues, men, women and children danced in streets, rang cowbells, blew horns and whistles, sang and shouted.

Opposite a dance hall at 140th Street and Lenox Avenue, where Louis had promised to make a personal appearance, more than 10,000 Negroes gathered for a glimpse of the fighter.

Another throng of 15,000 gathered near 140th and Seventh Avenue, where he was expected to pass. The police reported no disorder.

MIGRATIONS

As we have seen, the lives of Maya Angelou and her immediate family are characterized by a series of displacements. Born in St. Louis, Maya moves with her mother and father to California and is sent at the age of three from California to Arkansas to live with her grandmother. At the age of seven, Angelou is sent to live again with her mother, who has moved back to her hometown of St. Louis. Before moving in with their mother, Bailey and Maya live for half a year in St. Louis with their maternal grandparents. After she is raped, Maya and her brother are sent back to Arkansas. Later, when she is thirteen, Maya and Bailey travel with Momma to California. First they live with Momma in an apartment in Los Angeles for about six months. Then they move to Oakland, where their mother has an apartment. Finally they move to San Francisco when Vivian Baxter marries Daddy Clidell.

Although less is known about the movements of Maya's father, we know that he, too, leaves Arkansas, is in France during World War I, lives for a time with his wife and children in St. Louis, and eventually moves to California, where he works as a doorman at an expensive hotel and later in the kitchen of a naval hospital. Bailey Sr.'s movements are characteristic of the migration pattern of vast numbers of southern black men who moved from the rural South to urban areas north and west. In "The Present Status and Trends of the Negro Family," Charles S. Johnson notes the increasing urbanization of the black family:

> As late as 1890 the Negro population was 80 per cent rural; by 1920 the percentage had dropped to 66.0, and by 1930 to 56.3. At the present rate of urbanization this population will be more urban than rural in 1940. . . . In all of the southern states there is evidence of the disintegration of these culturally stagnant black belt communities, a spreading of the Negro population into southern towns and cities and, by long migration, to northern industrial centers. (249)

A U.S. Department of Labor study, *Negro Migration in 1916–17*, cites the following causes for the migration of large numbers of African Americans from the South during this period:

general dissatisfaction with conditions, ravages of boll weevil, floods, change of crop system, low wages, poor houses on plantations, poor school facilities, unsatisfactory crop settlements, rough treatment, cruelty of the law officers, unfairness in courts, lynching, desire for travel, labor agents, the Negro press, letters from friends in the North, and finally advice of white friends in the South where crops had failed. . . . However the influence came, and whatever concurrent causes may have operated, all will agree with Mr. Williams [a contributor to the report] when he says that "better wages offered by the North have been the immediate occasion for the exodus." (11–12)

The following excerpt from a report comparing black and white mobility patterns demonstrates that family and employment have played a major role in whether or not African Americans have migrated. Although the report does not deal directly with children, the reasons for Maya and Bailey's displacements are consistent with the important role played by family, while one may speculate that Bailey Sr.'s migrations were influenced by both family and employment opportunities.

EVA MUELLER AND WILLIAM LADD, *NEGRO-WHITE DIFFERENCES IN GEOGRAPHIC MOBILITY*
(U.S. Department of Commerce. Area Redevelopment Administration. Washington, D.C.: GPO, 1964)

The ties of the Negro to the community seem to be to an important extent family and friendship ties. Apparently the Negro migrant from the rural South, like the immigrant from Europe before him, often sent for or was followed by other members of his family. As a result we find that, even though only one-third of Negro adults are still living in the county where they were born 59 percent have all or most of their relatives living near them now in the same community. Most of the remaining Negro families reported that "some" relatives are living in the same community where they are. The survey shows that only 6 percent of Negro families, in contrast to 21 percent of white families, have no relatives in the community where they are now residing. It should be added that 48 percent of Negro families, but only 37 percent of white families, reported that *all* their close friends are living in their current place of residence. These contrasts between the Negro and the white populations are important since the survey shows that both past geographic mobility and moving plans are particularly low among families who have all or most of their relatives living near them.

When a family does decide to move, relatives may play a further role in facilitating and guiding the move. In discussing their most recent move across county lines, most Negro as well as most white families mentioned job or economic factors as the primary reason for moving. However, among Negroes who were born in the South and have moved North or West, family reasons were mentioned with considerable frequency. A third of this group said that they moved in order to be closer to a relative who had moved earlier. A closer look at cases of recent Negro migrants in the survey suggests that job and family considerations tend to be inseparable in many instances, since relatives are the major source of job information and often help the migrant to find work. For example:

- A 51 year-old Negro and his wife moved from Arkansas to California where their daughter and her family lived. The son-in-law told him he could get work there as a common laborer and in fact helped him to locate his first job as a janitor.

- A young Negro moved from Louisiana to the West Coast to join a brother who urged him to come. The brother then helped him to find a job in a shipyard by sending him to the appropriate union.

- A 30 year-old single Negro had moved from Kansas to California and had made several moves in California in an attempt to find suitable work. Then he heard that his father was in San Francisco and he joined him there. The father had an apartment and took him in until he had work; the father also took him around in his car to look for a job. He is now a waiter.

Similarly, in the case of return migrants to the South:

- A young Negro woman, domestic worker, who had been living in New York with her mother, returned to North Carolina when her mother died. All her other relatives were living in North Carolina.

- A middle-aged Negro born in the South had migrated to New York City in the early 1950's. In 1959 his boss died, and he became unemployed. He and his family returned to his wife's home town in the South. A friend there gave him a job as a farm laborer.

It seems then that family ties and emotional ties to a place and to friends are a greater barrier to mobility among Negro than among white families. Furthermore, such geographic moves that do occur, particularly among unskilled workers, in many instances seem to be guided by the location of relatives as much as by job opportunities. The role which relatives play in determining Negro moves may help to solve the difficult problems of adjustment to a new environment which the Negro migrant faces. But this system hardly provides an effective mechanism for guiding Negroes into areas of new opportunities or expanding employment.

Economic Incentives: The history of Negro migration during recent decades demonstrates clearly that the Negro population *does* move in response to strong economic incentives. According to Census data, the growing inadequacy of employment opportunities in Southern agriculture induced a net migration from the South of over 700,000 Negroes between 1920 and 1930. During the 1930's, when few job openings were beckoning, net Negro migration out of the South fell below 350,000. During the decade of World War II large numbers of job openings for unskilled workers at rising rates of pay led an unprecedented 1,200,000 Negroes to leave the South. The migration rate during World War II was higher for Negro than for white men; it was particularly high among unskilled Negro workers. We have noted already that since 1950 inter-county migration rates have been consistently lower for Negro than for white heads of families and that the Negro migration rate has declined while the rate for the white population has remained fairly constant. It is likely that the recent decline in the Negro migration rate reflects the growing deficiency of employment opportunities for unskilled workers. (17–20)

STUDY QUESTIONS

1. Discuss both the historical and contemporary roles of grandmothers in African American families.

2. What does Powdermaker mean when she writes of the "elasticity" of the African American family?

3. Why did mothers become the center of the African American family during slavery and after?

4. What factors contribute to the less dominant role in the family of the African American male as compared to the patriarchal orientation of white families?

5. Why did African Americans leave the South in large numbers in the first half of the twentieth century, and where did they go?

6. In what ways do the factors influencing the migration of African Americans differ from those that influence the migration of whites?

TOPICS FOR WRITTEN OR ORAL EXPLORATION

1. According to your reading of *I Know Why the Caged Bird Sings* and the documents in this chapter, is the importance of the extended family a strength or a weakness of the African American family?

2. Discuss the impact of Angelou's mother and father on her life as described in *I Know Why the Caged Bird Sings*. In what ways are Vivian Baxter's and Bailey Sr.'s behaviors (employment, marital status, role in their families) consistent with the historical dynamics of African American families as a result of slavery and a racist environment?

3. As a research project, trace the role of Vivian Baxter in her daughter's life, as recounted in the five volumes of Angelou's autobiography and in interviews she has given.

4. What similarities do you see between Angelou's description of her eighth-grade graduation and her description of Joe Louis's fight with Primo Carnera?

5. Why do you think Joe Louis was an important role model for African Americans? How does this compare to the importance of athletes as role models today?

6. Stage a debate in which the pros and cons of sports figures as role models are considered.

7. According to the documents in this chapter, in what ways are the various displacements of Maya and Bailey, as well as their parents' various

moves, consistent with the reasons for the migrations of other African Americans?

WORKS CITED

Angelou, Maya. *Gather Together in My Name*. New York: Random House, 1974.

———. *I Know Why the Caged Bird Sings*. 1970. Toronto: Bantam Books, 1971.

———. Interview with Stephanie Stokes Oliver. "Maya Angelou: The Heart of the Woman." *Essence* 14 (May 1983): 112–15.

———. Interview with Judith Paterson. "Interview: Maya Angelou—A Passionate Writer Living Fiercely with Brains, Guts, and Joy." *Vogue* (September 1982).

———. Interview with Dorothy Randall-Tsuruta. "An Interview with Maya Angelou." *Ambrosia* (October 1980): 3–8.

———. *Singin' and Swingin' and Gettin' Merry Like Christmas*. 1976. Toronto: Bantam Books, 1977.

Block, Maxine, ed. *Current Biography: Who's News and Why 1940*. New York: H. W. Wilson, 1940.

Frazier, E. Franklin. *The Negro Family in the United States*. Rev. and abr. ed. Chicago: University of Chicago Press, 1966.

Johnson, Charles S. "The Present Status and Trends of the Negro Family." *Social Forces* 16 (1937): 247–57.

Powdermaker, Hortense. *After Freedom: A Cultural Study in the Deep South*. 1939. Reprint. Madison: University of Wisconsin Press, 1993.

Shimkin, Demitri B., Edith M. Shimkin, and Dennis A. Frate, eds. "The Black Extended Family: A Basic Rural Institution and a Mechanism of Urban Adaptation." In *The Extended Family in Black Societies*. The Hague: Mouton, 1978.

Tate, Claudia, ed. *Black Women Writers at Work*. New York: Continuum, 1989.

U.S. Department of Labor. Division of Negro Economics. *Negro Migration in 1916–17*. Washington, D.C.: GPO, 1919.

SUGGESTED READINGS

See the full text of works excerpted in this chapter.

Elliot, Jeffrey M., ed. *Conversations with Maya Angelou*. Jackson: University Press of Mississippi, 1989.

For more on the African American family, see:

Frazier, E. Franklin. *The Negro Family in the United States*. Chicago: University of Chicago Press, 1939. (This first edition includes an extensive bibliography; the revised and abridged edition cited earlier does not.)

Gutman, Herbert G. *The Black Family in Slavery and Freedom, 1750–1925*. New York: Pantheon Books, 1976.

Heiss, Jerold. *The Case of the Black Family: A Sociological Inquiry*. New York: Columbia University Press, 1975.

Johnson, Charles S. *Shadow of the Plantation*. Chicago: University of Chicago Press, 1934.

Moynihan, Daniel. *The Case for National Action*. Washington, D.C.: GPO, 1965.

Rainwater, Lee, and William L. Yancey. *The Moynihan Report and the Politics of Controversy*. Cambridge, Mass: MIT Press, 1967.

For more on Joe Louis, see:

Van Deusen, John G. *Brown Bomber: The Story of Joe Louis*. Philadelphia: Dorrance, 1940.

Van Every, Edward. *Joe Louis: Man and Super-Fighter*. New York: Frederick A. Stokes, 1936.

For more on migration and urban life, see:

Coles, Robert. *The South Goes North: Volume III of Children of Crisis*. Boston: Little, Brown, 1967.

Drake, St. Clair, and Horace R. Cayton. *Black Metropolis: A Study of Negro Life in a Northern City*. Vols. 1 and 2. 1945. Rev. ed. New York: Harper and Row, 1962.

Henri, Florette. *Black Migration: Movement North, 1900–1920*. New York: Anchor Press, 1975.

6

Child Sexual Abuse

When asked whether any of her works have been misunderstood, Maya Angelou replied: "A number of people have asked me why I wrote about the rape in *I Know Why the Caged Bird Sings*. They wanted to know why I had to tell that rape happens in the black community" (Tate, 11). Indeed, this incident, which occurs in St. Louis when Maya is seven years old, is one of the most horrifying events of Angelou's childhood. But despite those who would criticize Angelou for revealing that child sexual abuse occurs in the African American community, studies have shown that child sexual abuse "is not limited by racial, ethnic, or economic boundaries—sexual abuse of children exists in all strata of society" (U.S. Department of Health and Human Services, i).

Angelou's account is a sensitive and brutally honest description of the abuse by her mother's boyfriend, Mr. Freeman, which progresses from fondling to forcible rape, and of her own confusion and pain as she tries to understand what is happening to her. The young Maya is frightened into submission by her abuser, as Mr. Freeman threatens to kill Bailey if Maya ever reveals the abuse. At the same time, however, Maya initially enjoys being held by Mr. Freeman. She writes, "From the way he was holding me I knew he'd never let me go or let anything bad ever happen to me" (61). After Mr. Freeman's crime is discovered, Maya is forced to testify in court against him. When asked whether Mr. Freeman had ever touched her before the rape, a guilt-ridden Maya lies and answers that he had not because she is afraid that she will be ostracized by her family if they find out that she had not disclosed his earlier fondling of her. Mr. Freeman is convicted and almost immediately found murdered. Maya, believing her lie makes her responsible for Mr. Freeman's death, decides that she must stop talking altogether so that others will not be harmed.

Angelou's account is consistent with many of the findings in current studies of child sexual abuse. Based on his survey of 796 college students, David Finkelhor reported that at least one of every five girls had had sexual experiences with substantially older partners and that "almost half [43%] of the girls' experiences were with family members" (57–58). Another 33% reported that the sexual experience occurred with an acquaintance. Angelou's experience is consistent with Finkelhor's contention that it is now a "well-established fact that sexual victimization occurs to a large extent within a child's intimate social network" (58). In regard to the age of the victim at the time of the sexual experience, Finkelhor notes: "It is assumed that a girl's vulnerability to sexual overtures increases as she acquires adult sexual characteristics. This assumption appears to be wrong, however. . . . Overall, experiences for both girls and boys cluster around the preadolescent period" (60). Finally, Finkelhor relates the victims' reactions to the sexual experience, the most common being fear or shock. However,

> a few (8 percent) actually remembered experiencing some pleasure as a result. . . . Contrary to the stereotype, most victims in our study readily acknowledged the positive as well as the negative elements of their experience. They talked about the times the physical sensations felt good, or they remembered how their sexual experience with an adult or family member satisfied a longing for affection and closeness that was rarely met at any other time.
>
> These were not expressions of adult kinds of sexual passion and longings. On the whole, they were part of a confusing flood of feelings and sensations, usually dwarfed by an overwhelming sense of helplessness, guilt, anger, or fear. In fact, the pleasure often only intensified the guilt or the helplessness, since it added to the child's confusion and left the child feeling out of control of even his or her own emotions. (65–66)

Angelou has stated that one of the challenges she faced in writing about the rape was to avoid portraying Mr. Freeman in a completely negative way. "I wanted people to see that the man was not totally an ogre" (Tate, 11). In an interview in 1987, Angelou commented on how she has been able to forgive Mr. Freeman: "It had to do . . . with 'seeing the man. I don't mean physically seeing him. But trying to understand how really sick and alone that man was. I don't mean that I condone at all. But to try to understand is always healing' " (Angelou, Interview with Crane, 175). Despite her ability to forgive, Angelou noted in this interview that she still bears the emotional scars of the abuse.

The following document, prepared for the National Center on Child Abuse and Neglect, helps to place Angelou's particular experience with sexual assault in the broader context of a significant national problem. It provides a definition of child sexual abuse, discusses the extent of the problem, analyzes the dynamics, and examines the effects of sexual abuse on children and families. The document relates directly to Angelou's case by demonstrating that sexual abuse is widespread, happens primarily to preadolescent girls, is often perpetrated by a male figure familiar to the child, and may have diverse short-term and long-term effects.

U.S. DEPARTMENT OF HEALTH AND HUMAN SERVICES, *CHILD SEXUAL ABUSE: INCEST, ASSAULT AND SEXUAL EXPLOITATION* (Rockville, Md: GPO, 1981)

Definitions

The sexual abuse of children has been called the "last remaining component of the maltreatment syndrome in children yet to be faced head on." It encompasses a wide range of behavior from fondling and exhibitionism to forcible rape and commercial exploitation for purposes of prostitution or the production of pornographic materials. It takes many forms and involves varying degrees of violence and emotional traumatization. Sexual abuse has been defined in a variety of ways. Some of the ambiguity in terms can be attributed to the differences in legal definitions of sexual abuse which vary considerably from state to state. But the basic cause of this ambiguity is the multitude of variations in sexual acts or behaviors, in perpetrators, and in the degree of harm or effect on children.

The Federal Child Abuse Prevention and Treatment Act of 1974, as amended, defines child abuse, including sexual abuse or exploitation, in terms of injury or maltreatment of a child "... by a person who is responsible for the child's welfare. ..." As used in Subsection 5(3) of the amended Act, the term "sexual abuse" includes "the obscene or pornographic photographing, filming or depiction of children for commercial purposes, or the rape, molestation, incest, prostitution or other such forms of sexual exploitation of children under circumstances which indicate that the child's health or welfare is harmed or threatened thereby ..."

Legal definitions of child sexual abuse sometimes vary by factors in addition to what was actually done to a child: the victim's age and relationship to the perpetrator are also taken into account in many states. Furthermore, because most child abuse reporting laws address themselves to maltreatment by parents or persons legally responsible for a child's welfare, an act of sexual abuse committed by a person outside the family may be defined and handled quite differently from the same act committed by someone legally responsible for the child.

As with other forms of child abuse, there is generally agreement concerning the most extreme cases, but the operational definition of what specific behaviors constitute sexual abuse of children remains largely a matter of jurisdictional and individual interpretation. Many of the terms in the literature that differentiate types of child sexual abuse are used interchangeably by professionals and the public. As more has become known about this problem, even such unintentional behaviors as obscene language or accidental sexual stimulus have been discussed as possibly constituting sexual abuse.

In order to encompass all forms of child sexual abuse and exploitation within its mandate, the National Center on Child Abuse and Neglect has adopted the following tentative definition of child sexual abuse:

> contacts or interactions between a child and an adult when the child is being used for the sexual stimulation of that adult or another person. Sexual abuse may also be committed by a person under the age of 18 when that person is either significantly older than the victim or when the abuser is in a position of power or control over another child.

Scope of the Problem

How frequently does child sexual abuse occur? The true extent of the problem is unknown, since there are presently no national statistics on the actual incidence of child sexual abuse. Available statistics reflect only those cases that are officially reported to appropriate authorities and represent only a fraction of the cases that actually occur. Some researchers believe that sexual abuse is more widespread than the physical abuse of children, which is currently estimated to affect over 200,000 children a year in the U.S. A study by Weinberg, published in 1955, estimated the average yearly rate of incest to be 1.9 cases per million people. More recent estimates have been considerably higher: in 1969, Vincent De-Francis, M.D., and the American Humane Association estimated a yearly incidence of about 40 per million. The number of cases seen at the Santa Clara County (California) Child Sexual Abuse Treatment Program suggests that the true incidence could be as high as 800 to 1,000 per million. The National Center on Child Abuse and Neglect currently estimates that the annual incidence of sexual abuse of children is over 100,000 cases per year.

For many researchers this incidence estimate is conservative. Authorities have offered a range of possible incidence figures, such as Schultz's estimate of 200,000–500,000 cases a year. In a study based on retrospective interviews with females, Gagnon estimated that as many as 500,000 girls under 14 years of age are victims of sexual offense each year. Another estimate within range of these assessments is Sarafino's projection of 336,000 actual sex offenses against boys and girls each year. In a recent survey of predominantly white, middle class college students, nearly one in five girls and one in 11 boys said they had a sexual experience with a much older person.

The variation among these estimates is primarily attributable to the methods employed in their computation. Such factors as the definition of sexual abuse utilized, the age range covered, and whether or not boys were included in the estimate are influential. . . .

There are a number of reasons to suppose that reported cases of sexual abuse represent only the "tip of the iceberg." One of these is the reluctance of many parents and family members to report such incidents to the authorities. Fear of social censure, shame, an unwillingness to subject the child and/or the parents to embarrassing questioning, and the fact that in most cases no physical harm has been done all contribute to this reluctance. Moreover, children often do not report incidents of sexual abuse to their parents. They may be afraid that their parents will blame them; they may be afraid of reprisal by the perpetrator (who may *be* one of their parents); or they may feel guilty over any physical pleasure they may have had from the sexual contact. In a retrospective study of 1,800 college students, almost a third of the respondents of both sexes reported that they had been subjected to some form of sexual abuse as children. Only half of the females who had such an experience reported it to their parents; only one tenth of the males did so. It is clear that the actual number of incidents of sexual abuse of children is considerably greater than the number of incidents that come to the attention of the authorities.

Dynamics of Sexual Abuse

The familiar images of "perverts," "molesters," and "dirty old men" are not accurate portraits of the majority of persons responsible for the sexual abuse of children. Studies of sexually abused children show that a large proportion of such cases involve parents or other figures familiar to the child. Of 9,000 cases of sex crimes against children reviewed by the American Humane Association in 1968, 75 percent were perpetrated by members of the victim's household, relatives, neighbors, or acquaintances of the victim. Half the offenders in a series of 42 cases involving sexual trauma of children and adolescents were found to be family members. . . . [Other studies] estimate that between 20 and 30 percent of all child abuse cases are perpetrated by nonfamily members. It has also been reported that only 3 to 10 percent of the offenders were total strangers.

The circumstances, dynamics, and effects of child sexual abuse differ depending on whether the perpetrator is a stranger or someone with whom the child is closely acquainted. The behavior of the perpetrator is more likely to be an expression of a sexual preference for children in cases of assault by a stranger than is that found in incest cases, where an individual's normal sexual preference for adults may have become thwarted, disoriented, or inappropriately directed toward a child. While aggressive sexual offenses, such as rape and sadism, do occur within the family, they are the exception rather than the rule. The majority of cases do not involve penetration, contraction of venereal disease, or infliction of serious injury. Exhibitionism and fondling by strangers, often compulsive and habitual forms of behavior, are rarely violent and may have little impact on their victims, depending upon how the situation is subsequently handled.

Sexual abuse by strangers is usually a single episode, occurs most frequently in the warm weather months, and usually occurs in a public place. In contrast, sexual abuse by family members or acquaintances is more likely to occur in the home of the victim or the perpetrator, and may occur repeatedly over a period of time.

While there are cases of sexual abuse by adult women, the overwhelming majority of perpetrators are men. Girls are reported as abused at a much higher rate than boys (the estimated ratio ranges from twice to ten times as often), and although victims have been found to be as young as four months old, the average age appears to be between 11 and 14 years old. Recent studies indicate, however, that these estimates may be more a reflection of the cases that are reported, rather than an actual indication of the age and sex of the majority of victims. For example, the 1978–79 statistics from the Child Protection Center of Children's Hospital National Medical Center, which treats all forms of child sexual abuse, reveal that the average age of victims is 7 years, and that 25 percent of them are males. Similarly, in a recent report by the Hennepin County (Minnesota) District Attorney's Office which identified previously undisclosed cases of child sexual abuse, as many boys as girls in the lower elementary school age levels identified themselves as having experienced some form of sexual abuse. These and similar data from other parts of the country increasingly point to the conclusion that, in younger children, as many boys as girls are vulnerable to sexual abuse and exploitation but that boys may be even more reluctant to report such incidents to adults. In addition, preliminary findings from the evaluation of NCCAN's four large intrafamily sexual abuse demonstration treatment projects indicate that 21 percent of the children being treated for sexual abuse are under the age of 12, with at least one project showing 51 percent of its child client population as 11 years old or younger, and one-third of its population under the age of six. . . .

There is evidence that most perpetrators of sexual abuse are heterosexual in their adult sexual orientation, even though they may abuse male children. Sarafino states that in 92 percent of the reported child sexual abuse cases the perpetrators are heterosexual. No perpetrators with a homosexual orientation were found in a study of 175 males convicted of sexual assault against children. The study suggests that the adult heterosexual male constitutes a greater risk to the underage male or female child than does the adult homosexual male (who is much less likely to have children around the house).

In cases where the perpetrator is a family friend or member, the use of physical force is rarely necessary to engage a child in sexual activity because of the child's trusting, dependent relationship with the perpetrator. The child's cooperation is often facilitated by the adult's position of dominance, an offer of material goods, a threat of physical violence, or a misrepresentation of moral standards. In complying with the adult's wishes, a child may also be attempting to fulfill needs that normally are met in other ways. For example, a child may cooperate out of a need for love, affection, attention, or from a sense of loyalty to the adult. Conversely, a need to defy a parental figure, express anger about a chaotic home life, or act out sexual conflicts may make a child vulnerable to sexual abuse and exploitation.

Other reports of child sexual abuse in the family suggest an elevated incidence of violence. In a study of 44 cases of attempted and completed child sexual assault by a family member, 39 percent of the offenders were categorized as committing a sex-pressure assault while 61 percent were categorized as committing a sex-force assault. In the sex-pressure assault the offender is an authority figure to the victim and pressures the child, who may not know that sexual activity is part of the offer. Sexual approaches by a family member are often presented to the child as instructional. Sex-force assaults, on the other hand, involve the threat of harm or physical force, rather than engaging the child in an emotional way. Intimidation and exploitation are used to gain power. In some cases this type of assault may be sadistic, where the child may be beaten, choked, or tortured, and where the intent of the perpetrator is to hurt, punish, or destroy the victim. . . .

Effects on Children and Families

It is difficult to generalize about the effects of sexual abuse on children. Aside from the fact that there has been little research on the effects of sexual abuse, children react differently to different situations depending on a number of variables that may be operating at the time of the occurrence. In an absolute sense, the question of what effects incest has had on the child is unanswerable since there is usually no way that the effects of the sexual events can be separated from the family pathology in which they occurred.

A number of factors are believed to be of critical importance in determining the way in which a child reacts to and assimilates the experience. These factors include the child's age and developmental status, the relationship of the abuser to the child, the amount of force or violence used by the abuser, the degree of shame or guilt evoked in the child for his or her participation, and, perhaps most importantly, the reactions of the child's parents and those professionals who become involved in the case. Most authorities agree that, other things being equal, the psychological trauma to the child is greater when the perpetrator of the abuse is close to the child than when he is a stranger (however, in a recent study by Finkelhor the connection between the degree of trauma and the relationship between victim and perpetrator was unclear). The closer the relationship between child and perpetrator, moreover, the more likely is the sexual abuse to be repeated.

It is not difficult to understand why some incidents of sexual abuse by a stranger may be far less traumatic than those committed by someone close to the child. In most such instances, the parents will rally to the aid of the child, and, while they may overreact to the situation, their anger and feelings of retribution are generally directed toward the perpetrator. It is less likely that provocation on the part of the child will be suspected, and the child will generally receive expressions of concern, protection, and support from family and friends. The degree of violence or physical coercion used by the perpetrator is, of course, another important factor:

if a child has been raped or otherwise physically harmed by an outsider, both the short- and long-term effects may be very serious.

Intrafamily sexual abuse, including that initiated by persons whom the child or other family members hold in high esteem, usually has far more complicated temporary and long-term repercussions. The public disclosure of incest may awaken feelings of guilt associated with denial and depression. If the mother has been aware of the situation, she may deny any knowledge of the matter, accusing her daughter of lying. The father's guilt, shame, and fear of retribution also may overwhelm any concern for his daughter's feelings. Thus, the child may be rejected by both parents, perceived as guilty, and seen as a betrayer of her family. Under these circumstances, many children retract their stories. Often, it is only after the incest is discovered that the larger family problems may surface (and vice versa).

The effects of incest also depend on the child's age and level of emotional and intellectual development. Very young children may be less affected by an incestuous relationship than older children, because they may not have incorporated society's concepts of right and wrong, and lack awareness of the possible repercussions. If the sexual behavior between adult and child has persisted over a long period of time, if it has involved a series of progressively more intimate incidents, or if the child is old enough to understand the cultural taboo of what has occurred, then the effects may be more profound.

Short-term effects of sexual abuse or its disclosure can take many forms. Some children react by regressing to earlier behaviors such as thumb sucking or becoming afraid of the dark; others sleep walk or develop difficulty in eating and sleeping. Sexual abuse may cause extreme anxiety which may be seen in excessive fears, enuresis, or tics. Such physical symptoms may constitute the child's way of acting out disturbing feelings and reactions that cannot be verbalized. A frequent symptom is the lack of inhibition of sexual impulses in the victim, who may seek love through sexual contact. Often, this behavior will result in the recurrence of sexual abuse to the child victim in the foster home.

Less is known about the long-term effects of incest and sexual exploitation because much of the research is clinical, based on small numbers of cases, and retrospective. Although retrospective studies have documented a relationship between reported incest history and the development of promiscuity or prostitution, other authors decry the use of ''failure to marry, or promiscuity'' as the only accepted criterion indicating that a victim has been harmed. The fact that many women reveal their incestuous history while involved in therapy for other problems, suggests that the damage from child sexual abuse may be related to other problems for which they are seeking help. Depression and confusion about their own identities are common reactions of many victims. Some jump into early marriages as a means of escaping their family situations and dealing with their feelings of aloneness. Some report feeling "marked" or stigmatized for life and may have suicidal tendencies. Many victims of incest come to the attention of the courts for antisocial behavior and may go through the entire justice system without ever revealing their underlying problems. There is no doubt, therefore, that in some cases incidents of child sexual abuse influence the personality and behavior of the victim for the rest of his or her life. Possible long-term effects include the repetition of self-destructive behavior patterns, such as drug or alcohol abuse, self mutilation, and the development of symptoms such as frigidity. (1–6)

STUDY QUESTIONS

1. Define the term "sexual abuse."

2. Why is sexual abuse an underreported crime?

3. What is the typical profile (sex, sexual orientation, familiarity with the victim) of the perpetrator of sexual abuse?

4. What is the typical profile (age and sex) of the victim of sexual abuse?

5. Why do children sometimes cooperate with the perpetrator of sexual abuse?

6. Families respond in a variety of ways when they learn a child has been sexually abused. Explain why and give some examples of possible reponses.

7. What are some of the short-term and long-term consequences for child victims of sexual abuse?

TOPICS FOR WRITTEN OR ORAL EXPLORATION

1. What were Angelou's objectives in writing about her experience with sexual abuse?

2. What were the short-term and long-term consequences for Angelou of the sexual abuse?

3. According to the studies cited in this chapter, in what ways was Angelou's experience similar to and different from the experiences of others who have suffered sexual abuse?

4. How did Angelou's family respond when they learned that she had been sexually abused? How does their response compare to the responses of other families in situations where the perpetrator was known to the family?

5. Write an essay, using supplementary materials, on ways to prevent child abuse.

6. Write and perform a dramatic sketch of a conversation between a parent and a child in which the parent prepares the child to protect himself or herself from sexual abuse.

WORKS CITED

Angelou, Maya. *I Know Why the Caged Bird Sings*. 1970. Toronto: Bantam Books, 1971.
———. Interview with Tricia Crane. "Maya Angelou." In *Conversations with Maya Angelou*. Ed. Jeffrey M. Elliot. Jackson: University Press of Mississippi, 1989. 173–78.

Finkelhor, David. *Sexually Victimized Children*. New York: The Free Press, 1979.

Tate, Claudia, ed. *Black Women Writers at Work*. New York: Continuum, 1983.

U.S. Department of Health and Human Services. *Child Sexual Abuse: Incest, Assault and Sexual Exploitation*. Rockville, Md.: GPO, 1981.

SUGGESTED READINGS

See the full text of *Child Sexual Abuse: Incest, Assault and Sexual Exploitation*. Many valuable resources on the topic of child sexual abuse are cited in the endnotes.

Fay, J. *He Told Me Not to Tell*. Renton, Wash.: King County Rape Relief, 1979.

Garbarino, James, and Gwen Gilliam. *Understanding Abusive Families*. Lexington, Mass.: Lexington Books, D. C. Heath, 1980.

Gilmartin, Pat. *Rape, Incest, and Child Sexual Abuse: Consequences and Recovery*. New York: Garland, 1994.

Iverson, Timothy J., and Marilyn Segal. *Child Abuse and Neglect: An Information and Reference Guide*. New York: Garland, 1990.

Pagelow, Mildred Daley. *Family Violence*. New York: Praeger, 1984.

Schetky, Diane H., et al. *Child Sexual Abuse: A Handbook for Health Care and Legal Professionals*. New York: Brunner/Mazel, 1988.

7

Censorship

Richard W. Beach and James D. Marshall provide the following definition of censorship in *Teaching Literature in the Secondary School*: "Censorship occurs when the government, or agents of the government, restricts access to information and resources. In schools, censorship occurs when School Boards prohibit specific titles, when administrators and department chairs forbid specific books, or when teachers decide not to assign a novel because the book might be considered controversial" (549).

According to Beach and Marshall, those who attempt censorship make certain assumptions about literary texts. They assume, first, "that 'fiction' and reality are the same" and will therefore challenge texts that they think will have a negative effect on real-life beliefs and conduct. Second, censors assume that reading literary texts can cause changes in beliefs and conduct, "that if adolescents read what are perceived to be portrayals of 'objectionable' behavior—sex, drug use, violence, profane language use, then their attitudes and behaviors will be changed in a predictable direction." Third, censors believe that it is possible and necessary to create a teaching environment that is "value-free." Finally, those who attempt censorship have a narrow view of adolescents, seeing them as "innocent, passive victims who, because they are not mature enough to develop their own values, need to be protected" (550, 551).

In *Banned in the U.S.A.*, Herbert N. Foerstel suggests that the problem of censorship is not new, noting, somewhat facetiously, that "the issue of banned books has been escalating since Johannes Gutenberg introduced the printing press in 1455" (xi). Foerstel traces the history of censorship and finds that many of the issues involved in earlier centuries remain the same today: "As we approach the twenty-first century, faith and fear are still prominent in determining our right to free expression" (xiii).

Certainly in recent years, Angelou's *I Know Why the Caged Bird Sings* has been the target of many censorship attacks motivated by "faith and fear." In 1995 it was the "most challenged" book in the United States, according to the American Library Association's Office for Intellectual Freedom ("Maya Angelou's 'Most Challenged' Book"). The objections to Angelou's book are many and varied. Some censors have challenged it because they believe that Angelou promotes hatred in her attitude toward whites; others have objected to profane language; still others have claimed that the book is anti-religion. Most of the censorship attacks, however, have centered on sexually explicit content, particularly the rape scene.

The following documents explore the issue of censorship in general as well as specific incidents of attempted censorship of *I Know Why the Caged Bird Sings*. The first document, published by People for the American Way, provides a general analysis of the trends identified in a recent annual survey of censorship. The second document, an excerpt from the *Banned Books Week Resource Guide, 1997*, published by the American Library Association's Office for Intellectual Freedom, summarizes some of the specific objections made to *I Know Why the Caged Bird Sings* since 1983. This is followed by a group of documents describing six recent incidents of censorship or attempted censorship of *I Know Why the Caged Bird Sings*. The final documents provide an in-depth case study of one recent incident of attempted censorship of Angelou's autobiography in Lawrence County, Alabama.

TRENDS IN CENSORSHIP ATTACKS

People for the American Way is a nonpartisan constitutional liberties organization that provides technical and legal assistance to educators and citizens to help prevent or defeat censorship attempts. In addition, the organization conducts research and publishes an annual survey documenting censorship attempts and other relevant challenges to public education. The information is gathered from teachers, librarians, school officials, parents, and students who have been involved in an incident.

The following excerpt from the organization's 1996 survey discusses the frequency of censorship attacks, the targets of these attacks, the groups responsible for the majority of attempts to censor, and the basis for their objections. It is significant that objections to sexual content account for 44 percent of the complaints, in that offensive sexual content is a leading reason given by those who have sought to censor *I Know Why the Caged Bird Sings*. In addition, it is noteworthy that African American women writers like Angelou have been the subject of a disproportionate number of attacks and that People for the American Way sees these attacks as part of a broader assault on multicultural education.

ATTACKS ON THE FREEDOM TO LEARN: 1996 REPORT
(Washington, D.C.: People for the American Way, 1996)

While attacks on public education occurred with increasing frequency, actual censorship and attempts to censor have given way to broader assaults on the public schools. Objections were leveled at classroom and library books, health and sexuality education programs, student newspapers and literary magazines, field trips, plays, school reform efforts, optional counseling services and more. At the same time, anti-education groups and individuals have broadened their focus to include voucher legislation, attempts to inject prayer and religion into the public schools, personal attacks on teachers and administrators, and a renewed fight to add Creationism to science classes. Overall, censorship continues to threaten America's schoolchildren, but its destructive impact is being matched by a new wave of ideological assaults on public education.

Attacks overall are on the rise: During the 1995–96 school year, there were more attempts to remove or restrict educational materials, censor school programs, stifle student expression, pass harmful, anti–public education legislation and inject coercive religious doctrine into the official school day than ever before in the 14-year history of this report. Researchers confirmed 475 incidents in 44 states in all regions of the country. Those 475 incidents include both outright attempts to censor materials, as well as efforts to impose an ideological or sectarian agenda through other means. States with the highest number of incidents were California, Pennsylvania and Florida. No incidents, however, were reported in Arkansas, Delaware, Hawaii, North Dakota, Vermont, West Virginia or Wyoming.

Censorship and its success rate: Censorship continues to be a serious problem in the public schools and remains the single most common practice of opponents of public education in their efforts to impose ideological, political or religious agendas on the nation's classrooms. While the number of reported censorship attempts has decreased, reaching 300 during the 1995–96 school year, censorship is only one tactic among many employed by those seeking to control the public schools. In a positive development, the success rate of would-be censors decreased somewhat this year, dropping to 41 percent, still disturbingly high, but lower than last year's record high of 50 percent.

Scope of challenges continues to widen: In what is the most alarming finding of the report this year, the number of broad-based challenges to public education increased by 46 percent, rising from last year's record level of 120 to 175 this year. These complaints include campaigns to inject state-coerced school prayer or other religious activity into the official school day, attempts to include Creationism in biology classes, challenges to school reform, and efforts to enact a school voucher plan or pass so-called parental rights legislation that will effectively undermine the quality of public education. In many communities, Religious Right political groups are either spearheading or supporting these efforts as an extension of their censorship activity.

No area of public education was left unaffected: Virtually no aspect of the curriculum is safe from attempted censorship, from student newspapers to science classes, from library collections to kindergarten picture books.

Library materials were frequent targets: Thirty seven percent of all censorship attempts were leveled at school library materials, books no child is required to read. Even more disturbing are the number of incidents in which no particular titles were challenged, but instead objectors simply sought to "cleanse" whole collections of books that discuss sex or contain otherwise offensive material.

African American women authors under siege: A disproportionate number of books written by African American women were attacked this year, with Maya Angelou's *I Know Why the Caged Bird Sings* being the most frequently challenged book in the country. These assaults reflect a broader attack on multicultural education and efforts to make history and English curricula more accurate and complete by including contributions of women and minorities.

Religious Right political groups lead the charge: Sixteen percent of the incidents reported directly involved national, state or local Religious Right political organizations. An additional 16 percent appeared to be coordinated or inspired by these same extremist groups. Religious Right political leaders have long targeted public education, and the movement is at the forefront of censorship attempts and other assaults on public education in America's schools. This year, the Christian Coalition and its activists have been particularly active in their anti-education efforts, often from seats on school boards, and they have been at the center of controversies ranging from the censorship of public citizens during the public comment period of school board meetings to objecting to sexuality education materials.

Objections based on sexual content, objectionable language and religion most frequent: The most frequent complaint lodged against challenged materials was that the treatment of sexuality was found to be offensive. That charge was leveled against 131 challenged materials, a full 44 percent of all censorship complaints. This unprecedented figure marks a significant increase over last year's figure of 33 percent. Second most common were challenges in which materials were deemed to be profane or to contain otherwise objectionable language. The third most common were those in which materials were perceived to be at odds with the objector's religious beliefs.

Anti-gay objections on the rise: For the second year in a row, challenges involving claims that educators were attempting to "promote" homosexuality reached record numbers. Eighteen percent of all challenges, 85 in all, up from nearly 16 percent last year, stemmed from such accusations.

Sex education controversies: Sex education controversies continued to soar during the 1995–1996 school year. Controversies occurred in 92 communities across the nation, up from 62 similar incidents last year.

Student newspapers, school plays and magazines continued to be a prime target: These challenges to student expression are particularly disturbing, in that they represent an attempt to halt students' creativity and critical thinking about the world around them. (5–7)

CENSORSHIP OF *I KNOW WHY THE CAGED BIRD SINGS*

The American Library Association's Office for Intellectual Freedom was established in 1967 to educate both librarians and citizens about the importance of intellectual freedom in libraries. It publishes the *Banned Books Week Resource Guide*, which lists books that have been challenged or banned. The entry for *I Know Why the Caged Bird Sings* follows. Based on information reported in the bimonthly *Newsletter on Intellectual Freedom*, it includes the year and location of each challenge to the work since 1983 on which the organization has information. (The American Library Association notes that many incidents of censorship go unreported.) In some cases, the stated reasons for the challenge and the outcome are also given.

The document gives a general idea of the types of challenges to which *I Know Why the Caged Bird Sings* has been subject. Later documents provide details about specific incidents. Taken together, they offer insight into the breadth and depth of the attempts to censor *I Know Why the Caged Bird Sings* and allow us to draw our own conclusions about the trends and themes which these challenges reveal.

BANNED BOOKS WEEK RESOURCE GUIDE, 1997
(Chicago: Office for Intellectual Freedom, American Library
Association, 1997)

Angelou, Maya. *I Know Why the Caged Bird Sings*. Bantam. Four members of the Alabama State Textbook Committee (1983) called for its rejection because Angelou's work preaches "bitterness and hatred against whites." Challenged at Mount Abram Regional High School in Strong, Maine (1988) because parents objected to a rape scene. Rejected as required reading for a gifted ninth grade English class in Bremerton, Wash. (1990) because of the book's "graphic" description of molestation. Removed from a Banning, Calif. eighth grade class (1991) after several parents complained about explicit passages involving child molestation and rape. Challenged at the Amador Valley High School in

Pleasanton, Calif. (1992) because of sexually explicit language. Temporarily banned from the Caledonia Middle School in Columbus, Miss. (1993) on the grounds that it is too sexually explicit to be read by children. Challenged in the Haines City, Fla. High School library and English curriculum (1993) because of objections to a passage that describes the author's rape when she was seven years old. Challenged in the Hooks, Tex. High School in a freshman honors history class (1993). Retained as required reading for all of Dowling High School's sophomores in Des Moines, Iowa (1994). The book became an issue after a parent objected to what he said were inappropriately explicit sexual scenes. Challenged as part of the Ponderosa High School curriculum in Castle Rock, Colo. (1994) because it is "a lurid tale of sexual perversion." Challenged at the Westwood High School in Austin, Tex. (1994) because the book is pornographic, contains profanity, and encourages premarital sex and homosexuality. The superintendent later ruled that parents must first give their children permission to be taught potentially controversial literature. Challenged at the Carroll School in Southlake, Tex. (1995) because it was deemed "pornographic" and full of "gross evils." Challenged, but retained on the Beech High School reading list in Hendersonville, Tenn. (19[9]5). Challenged at the Danforth High School in Wimberley, Tex. (1995). Removed from the Southwood High School Library in Caddo Parish, La. (1995) because the book's language and content were objectionable. Eventually, the book was returned after students petitioned and demonstrated against the action. Challenged, but retained in the Volusia County, Fla. County Schools (1995). The complainants wanted the book removed because "it is sexually explicit and promotes cohabitation and rape." Challenged, but retained on an optional reading list at the East Lawrence High School in Moulton, Ala. (1996). The book was challenged because the School Superintendent decided "the poet's descriptions of being raped as a little girl were pornographic." Removed from the curriculum pending a review of its content at the Gilbert, Ariz. Unified School (1995). Complaining parents said the book did not represent "traditional values." Retained on the Round Rock, Tex. Independent High School reading list (1996) after a challenge that the book was too violent. Pulled from the reading list at Lakota High School in Cincinnati, Ohio (1996) because of parents' claims that it is too graphic. Source: 7, Mar. 1983, p. 39; Jan. 1989, p. 8; Mar. 1989, p. 38; Nov. 1990, p. 211; Mar. 1992, p. 42; July 1992, p. 109; July 1993, p. 107; Jan. 1994, p. 34; July 1994, p. 130; Jan. 1995, pp. 11, 14; Mar. 1995, p. 56; May 1995, pp. 67, 72; Sept. 1995, pp. 158–59; Nov. 1995, pp. 183, 186–87; Jan. 1996, pp. 14, 30; Mar. 1996, pp. 47, 63; May 1996, pp. 84, 99; July

1996, p. 120; Sept. 1996, pp. 152–53; Nov. 1996, pp. 197–98; Jan. 1997, p. 26.

This group of documents concerns incidents of censorship or attempts to censor *I Know Why the Caged Bird Sings* reported by People for the American Way in 1996. Each of the six selections summarizes an incident, identifies the objector, and discusses the resolution of the case. These entries demonstrate that censorship continues to be a threat to education in the United States.

The specifics of each incident provide further insight into the nature of the objections, while the information provided about the resolutions to each case details a variety of responses to the challenges. Readers can evaluate the rate of success of the challenges and the appropriateness of the responses to the challenges. In some cases, the information also allows readers to analyze the effectiveness of a particular school's policies and procedures for dealing with censorship.

ATTACKS ON THE FREEDOM TO LEARN: 1996 REPORT
(Washington, D.C: People for the American Way, 1996)

INCIDENT: In Boise [Idaho], objections to *I Know Why the Caged Bird Sings* by Maya Angelou, used in the ninth grade, for being too sexually explicit. The objector claimed the book "heightens the decaying morals of our youth." Removal requested.
OBJECTOR: Parent.
RESOLUTION: The book has been removed from the junior high curriculum, but is to be used at the high school level. This decision withstood a series of appeals by the objector. The first two committees to review the book found it appropriate for the grade level at which it was being used, while the last committee, made up of the four quadrant directors for the district, decided the book would be more appropriate on the high school reading list. (122–23)

INCIDENT: In Decatur [Illinois], objections to *I Know Why the Caged Bird Sings* by Maya Angelou, in use in a ninth-grade enriched language arts class, for containing a descriptive rape scene. The objector called the book "garbage," "trash and pervertedness" and "pornographic" and objected that the book did not describe the rape scene as "abnormal, child molestation, or 'a crime.' " Removal requested.
OBJECTOR: Parent.

RESOLUTION: After the objector wrote a letter to the school board, a review committee recommended retaining the book in the language arts curriculum. As part of its evaluation, the committee used several professional recommendations in defense of the book, including the American Library Association's *Booklist*, which has recommended *I Know Why the Caged Bird Sings* for 14- to 18-year-olds three times since it was published in 1970. The committee further stated that parents have the right to reject books they deem unsuitable for their children and can request that their children be given an alternative assignment.

While the superintendent supported the committee's recommendation, he issued a directive that parents must be notified before the book can be used in the future. In this instance, the teacher had sent home a notification slip, informing parents of the book's content and notifying them that an alternate assignment was available. Next year, he will distribute permission slips that encourage parents to read the book before giving their children permission to read it. (126–27)

INCIDENT: In Shawnee Mission [Kansas], objections to *I Know Why the Caged Bird Sings* by Maya Angelou, available in an eighth-grade English class, for allegedly being "absolutely inappropriate material for secondary level students," full of "pornographic and violent material . . . which is anything but academic by nature" and using the word "nigger." "At this stage of their life they will only be able to identify with the promiscuity and indecent tantalizing scenes. Material such as this, can NOT make them mature faster and has no place in school," stated the objector. Removal requested.

OBJECTOR: Parent, representing herself and a "growing number of concerned parents."

RESOLUTION: The review committee unanimously agreed that the book was "appropriate for student in-class instruction in grades eight through twelve and appropriate to be available for student checkout in libraries at the middle and high school levels." The objector filed the request for removal after her child opted out of the assignment as per school policy. The decision to retain the book was reached in October of 1995, yet the objector was still complaining to the local media in April of 1996.

The objector also appeared before the school board advocating the teaching of Creationism and the adoption of the pro-Creationist text *Of Pandas and People*. The objector also petitioned for guest speakers in American history classes, whom she describes as "conservative historians," to teach students "the true meaning of the Constitution." She was unsuccessful. (144)

INCIDENT: In Portage [Michigan], objections to *Beloved* by Toni Morrison and *A Yellow Raft in Blue Water* by Michael Dorris, in use in a ninth-grade honors English class, and *I Know Why the Caged Bird Sings* by Maya Angelou, in use in a tenth-grade English class, for containing "inappropriate language" that dealt with rape, bestiality and a "graphic sex scene in a public place." Removal requested.
OBJECTOR: Parents.
RESOLUTION: A review committee voted to retain *Caged Bird* in the tenth grade, but to move the other two books to a higher grade level after this year. The committee felt that *Beloved* and *A Yellow Raft in Blue Water* were "too mature for the [ninth-grade] age level." For this year, the two books were moved from the required to the optional reading list and the children of the objectors were offered alternate reading assignments for all three books. (170–71)

INCIDENT: In Wildwood [New Jersey], objections to *I Know Why the Caged Bird Sings* by Maya Angelou, in use in a tenth-grade English class, for sexual content. Removal requested.
OBJECTOR: Parent.
RESOLUTION: The objector filed a formal complaint against the book, but agreed to have his child read an alternate assignment before a board committee was formed to review the book. During the challenge, a school official read several passages of the book, and, while he thought "some of it was graphic," he said he would prefer to have his teenage daughter learn about issues of sexuality with the aid of a skilled teacher rather than on her own. (204–5)

INCIDENT: In Round Rock [Texas], objections to *Winter in the Blood* by James Welch, *The Power of One* by Bryce Courtenay, *House Made of Dawn* by Scott Momaday, *Beloved* by Toni Morrison, *I Know Why the Caged Bird Sings* by Maya Angelou, *Bless Me Ultima* by Rudolpho Anaya, *Black Boy* by Richard Wright, *Ceremony* by Leslie Marmon Silko, *The Color Purple* by Alice Walker, *A Thousand Acres* by Jane Smiley, *Native Son* by Richard Wright, and *Slaughterhouse Five* by Kurt Vonnegut, on elective reading lists at two high schools, for containing violence and sexual situations. Removal from the reading lists requested.
OBJECTOR: School board trustee.
RESOLUTION: At a boisterous seven-hour meeting attended by nearly 300 parents, teachers and students, the school board voted 4–2 to reject the proposal to remove the books from the reading lists. More than 100 parents, students and teachers were scheduled to speak at the meeting, most of whom were opposed to the trustee's proposal and decried it as

censorship. One student said, "The whole thing is motivated by fear. They're afraid that we're actually going to have to think for ourselves." A teacher compared judging the books only by their provocative excerpts to judging Michelangelo's "David" exclusively on the sculpture's genitals. But parents supporting the ban insisted that the proposal did not amount to censorship. "It's deciding what is consistent with society's standards and appropriate for everyone to use in the classroom," said one.

Other members of the community argued that a minority of vocal parents was trying to impose its standard of decency on the rest of the community and suggested that the proposal is linked to a broader attempt to squelch multicultural curricula in the schools, noting that nine of the 12 books were written by minority authors. Said one citizen, "It's a concerted attempt to eliminate studies of communities or ethnicities that are different than what they grew up with."

If it had passed, the proposal would have circumvented a review system implemented during the 1994–95 school year in response to an unsuccessful challenge to *I Know Why the Caged Bird Sings* by Maya Angelou. That review system provides parents with an annotated book list and a permission slip at the beginning of each school year. This process alerts parents to books with violent or sexual content and enables them to restrict their children from reading books they deem inappropriate. While those who supported the books' removal criticized the annotated list saying that the book descriptions were not detailed enough, those opposed to the ban insist that the current method offers parents ample opportunities to withhold individual selections from their children. (276)

The following newspaper articles from the *Decatur Daily* provide an in-depth case study of an attempt to ban *I Know Why the Caged Bird Sings* at East Lawrence High School in Lawrence County, Alabama. They trace the controversy from its beginnings in November 1995 to its conclusion in October 1996.

The case began when a parent complained to the superintendent of schools, Patrick Graham, about material in *I Know Why the Caged Bird Sings*. Upon examining the passages in question, Graham deemed them "pornographic." Rather than following approved procedures for a review of reading materials, the superintendent unilaterally decided that the book would be banned from the list of outside reading material for Ernestine Robinson's ninth-grade students. Robinson objected to Graham's actions and took her case to the Lawrence County Board of Education, where Graham argued that he banned the book because of Angelou's description of the rape by her mother's boyfriend and other sexually explicit material. Following the board of education meeting, a parent, George F. Thomas, then complied with school procedure for book banning by filing a form with the school's media committee. (One article outlines the procedure for banning a book in Lawrence County.) A March newspaper account of the debate on Thomas's complaint details some of the arguments of the would-be censors and the opponents of the ban.

The school media committee decided not to ban *I Know Why the Caged Bird Sings*, but rather chose to make it required reading for all high school honors, advanced placement, and pre–advanced placement English classes, and to keep the book on the supplemental reading list for all other English classes. Following this decision, teachers who had opposed the ban reported that they were being harassed. Unhappy with the decision, Thomas took his appeal to the next level, the Lawrence County School System Media Committee. The *Decatur Daily*'s coverage of the second hearing again details the arguments of both sides of the debate. The county school system media committee responded by deciding that *I Know Why the Caged Bird Sings* could be assigned by any teacher in grades nine through twelve, but that a book of comparable literary value would have to be made available to students whose parents objected to it. Still not satisfied, Thomas appealed to the county school board. The school board voted 3–2 against the book's removal, thus ending the debate and letting stand the county media committee's decision.

The newspaper coverage of this case demonstrates the emotionalism that can surround a controversy such as this. The case is noteworthy in that it shows the tenacity of would-be censors and provides insight into the arguments used to justify positions both for and against censorship. The case's outcome suggests that it is important for school systems to have policies and procedures for dealing with censorship attempts and that courage and determination equal to that of those who attempt censorship are necessary in order to respond to their actions. (Portions of later articles have been omitted to avoid needless repetition.)

LESLEY FARREY PACEY, " 'CAGED BIRD' BAN ANGERS TEACHER:
ANGELOU BOOK SHUT WITHOUT APPROVAL OF BOARD,
TEACHER SAYS"
(*Decatur Daily* [Decatur, Alabama], November 21, 1995, C1+)

MOULTON—An East Lawrence High School teacher said Superintendent
Patrick Graham violated school board policy when he banned a book her
students were reading. The school board said nothing.

Language arts teacher Ernestine Robinson also demanded a public
apology from Graham for "questioning her ethics" in allowing her ninth-
grade students to read "I Know Why the Caged Bird Sings," an autobiography by Maya Angelou.

The critically acclaimed poet and author writes in her autobiography
about the trials and joys of a black girl growing up in Stamps, Ark. But
she may be best known for her poem at President Clinton's inauguration
three years ago.

"On Monday, Graham came to school using Gestapo tactics, saying this
book is not to be used, period," Ms. Robinson said at a 3 ½-hour
Lawrence County Board of Education meeting Monday night.

Ms. Robinson said students and parents have been "clamoring 'What's
wrong?' " About half of the 60-member audience clapped when she asked
for an apology.

The board policy states that any employee of the school system may
object to reading materials, but must complete an appeal form and bring
that concern to a media committee. Any action taken related to the materials "must be taken by the appropriate media committee and not by
an individual," the policy reads.

Special meetings may be called by the principal or superintendent to
consider temporary removal of materials in unusual circumstances, the
policy states. But temporary removal "shall require a majority vote by the
committee."

"This is your approved policy," she said. "If you are going to have
harmony, you can't have people galloping out on their own, dismissing
books, saying it did not fit the classroom."

But Graham argued he has a right to override board policy. He said he
has no intention of apologizing to Ms. Robinson.

"I am not going to apologize for keeping our kids from reading the
material contained in that book or any other—no matter how much it is
approved—if it is explicitly pornographic in nature," Graham said.

Graham, who often hands out pocket-sized Bibles to school system
visitors, said he asked East Lawrence High School Principal K. C. Thomaskutty to pull Ms. Angelou's book after parents brought some "por-

nographic" sections of the book to his attention. He said this is the first time he ever banned a book.

"When I looked at the book, I agreed that I didn't want children reading a book where someone seduced someone sexually," Graham said.

He points to two scenes in particular. The book describes a scene where the 8-year-old Angelou is raped by her mother's boyfriend.

In another scene, Angelou talks about "seducing a young boy," Graham said.

"I will be against that until I can't take another breath," he said.

LESLEY FARREY PACEY, "WHO KNOWS WHY 'CAGED BIRD' IS SINGLED OUT? EAST LAWRENCE PARENT TO PURSUE BAN" (*Decatur Daily*, December 10, 1995, B1+)

CADDO—Two English teachers at East Lawrence High School are pleased an attempt to ban Maya Angelou's autobiography is going through the proper procedure for book banning.

East Lawrence parent George F. Thomas said he will be filing a form with the school's media committee to remove "I Know Why the Caged Bird Sings" from outside reading for ninth-graders because it is too sexually explicit. He declined to comment on the record.

Meanwhile, ninth-grade students who want to can continue reading the book, an optional assignment to begin with, said English teacher Ernestine Robinson.

"I've told kids who chose to read it to go ahead," she said. "Kids who did not want to read it or whose parents don't want them to read it don't have to. I did not want to twist anyone's arm."

Mrs. Robinson said she's ignored Superintendent Patrick Graham's attempt to remove the book last month because "it was illegally lifted."

Graham admits he didn't follow the school board policy on book bans, which required the filing of a formal complaint and a series of reviews.

Mrs. Robinson said she's glad Thomas is filing a formal complaint. "That is fine, that is what I wanted to be done. But it in no way exonerates the superintendent."

Graham said he told the school's principal, K. C. Thomaskutty, to remove the book in November after parents brought some "pornographic" sections of the book to his attention.

"We want it [the ban] to be done in a logical, democratic manner, rather than a demagogic type atmosphere," said Mrs. Robinson.

"If it goes through all the proper channels and they find something wrong with it, then that's another thing," said Anita Bowling, chairwoman of the school's English Department and president of Lawrence County Language Arts Teachers Association. "It just needs to go through the proper channels."

She said the process is a good one because the burden of proof is on the person trying to remove the book. "They must show they read it and they must be specific."

Mrs. Robinson finds irony, however, in the timing of the attempted book ban.

"Right down the road we have a rape, but we are not permitted to read about rape in class," she told a ninth-grade class, referring to a newspaper article about arrests in what authorities say was a Dec. 2 gang rape in North Courtland. "It's a grisly article, but life is sometimes what, students?"

"Grisly," she said, answering her rhetorical question.

Graham said Ms. Angelou's account of her childhood should be removed because she described being raped as a child by her mother's boyfriend and other passages about sexuality. The book recounts what it was like growing up as a black female in rural Arkansas in the 1930s.

Mrs. Robinson said students learned about Ms. Angelou because an excerpt from the book is the first reading in the ninth-grade English textbook. The poet's picture is on the cover.

"It whetted their appetite for more," she said.

Students who wanted to read the book paid for their copies and Mrs. Robinson ordered about 100. Mrs. Robinson said a ban of the book is an affront to the author, a Reynolds Professor at Wake Forest University in North Carolina, who read her poem "On the Pulse of the [sic] Morning" at President Bill Clinton's inauguration in 1993.

"I attribute it to ignorance and male dominance, even though the educational professional basis in this county is predominantly female," she said.

But mostly, she doesn't want the book removed because she feels it is valuable to students. "Public education is like an open forum for kids to sop up every bit of knowledge to fight the foes they meet in their adult lives."

"One student I had went through this [being raped as a child]," said Mrs. Bowling. "Because of this book, she has been able to open up with it. This is in the world. It's not a perfect world."

Two of Mrs. Robinson's ninth-grade students said they will continue reading the book.

"I think students can handle it because you see it every day," said ninth-grader Margaret Sears.

"I can handle it," said one ninth-grader, who didn't want his name used because his parents did not approve of the book. "My mom thinks some of the kids are not mature enough to read it, but I'm going to read it anyway."

Both Mrs. Robinson and Mrs. Bowling said they have assigned the book for several years with no problem. Mrs. Bowling said she knows of only two other attempts to ban books in Lawrence County, but they occurred at other schools involving different books.

[The following inset accompanied the preceding article:]

"HOW TO BAN A BOOK"
(*Decatur Daily*, December 10, 1995, B1+)

Lawrence County School Board policy states that anyone who objects to reading materials, must complete an appeal form and appear before a media committee.

These are the steps that must be followed to officially ban "I Know Why the Caged Bird Sings."

- Appearance before East Lawrence High School's Media Committee. Its members are Principal K. C. Thomaskutty, the library media specialist, one teacher from each appropriate grade area, a student and school parents equal to the number of school employees. The media specialist makes appointments. Two English teachers who use the book, Anita Bowling and Ernestine Robinson, are on the committee.

- The committee may decide to ban the book from all grades or certain grades or reject the ban.

- The committee's decision can be appealed to the Lawrence County Media Committee appointed by Superintendent Patrick Graham.

- The last step is an appeal to the Lawrence County Board of Education.

The written appeal form for non-fiction reading material considers the purpose, authenticity, appropriateness and content of the book and previous reviews done on the book.

LESLEY FARREY PACEY, "EAST LAWRENCE DEBATES BAN ON
ANGELOU'S BOOK"
(*Decatur Daily*, March 13, 1996, A1+)

CADDO—One woman quoted Bible verses and told a school media committee they would "have to answer to God" if they didn't ban Maya Angelou's autobiography.

Another woman said sexual deviants are born from reading passages like those contained in "I Know Why the Caged Bird Sings."

"When [serial killer] Ted Bundy was a child he was introduced to soft-core porn, and he had good parents," said parent and church youth director Peggy McCleskey.

"Through something he saw and read, he was held captive the rest of his life. This might fall on the minds of children who can't cope. How do you know we don't have a Ted Bundy [in school]?"

Many of the 40 people filling a [*sic*] East Lawrence High School classroom for a hearing Tuesday night said they didn't want their high school students reading the critically acclaimed author and poet's book. Others nodded in agreement.

But the group likely won't know until next week if the book will be removed from outside reading for ninth-grade students. A 12-member committee will give its decision first to parent George F. Thomas who complained about the book in December. The book was an optional reading assignment for students who could choose other books. English teachers at the school have used the book for 20 years. This is the first attempt to ban it from the county reading list.

Thomas filed the complaint after Superintendent Patrick Graham, acting in violation of school board policy, attempted to ban the book himself. Thomas said certain passages are sexually explicit. At the hearing, he detailed sexual scenes in the book and muttered "this is ridiculous" after the committee held him to a five-minute time limit for speakers.

"If these scenes were in a movie they would be rated X or at least NC-17," said Thomas. ". . . These are things that the adolescent mind does not need to be subjected to." . . .

Nine of the 13 people who spoke at the hearing—including parents, pastors and Sunday school teachers—said they didn't want their children reading sexual passages and were offended by "profane" language in the book. Most said Ms. Angelou's account of being raped as a child by her mother's boyfriend and other passages about sexuality were too descriptive. Some cried and trembled as they spoke.

"It's a 'How To' manual," Ms. McCleskey said. "It shows how to arouse, seduce and rape one's victim."

Defending the book were a teacher and three advanced English students—including the son of a preacher. All four said they are Christians, but the book . . . shouldn't be removed.

East Lawrence biology teacher Michelle Cleveland told the group that the book teaches students "that good things can come from bad things." She said many students likely can relate to Ms. Angelou's experiences of being poor and black in the South, bounced back and forth to different relatives' homes and some may have been molested.

"Without those poignant scenes, Maya could not convey the truth about her life," Ms. Cleveland said.

Clad in a baseball uniform, East Lawrence senior Clint Jones said he is the son of a preacher and the book is one of the best he's read. He urged parents not to shelter their children from "real-world" truths no matter how ugly.

"Don't try to build this wall around your children," said Jones, who recently got a college football scholarship. "My parents tried to protect me from things and when I got out in the real world, it was a shock and I took some wrong turns because of that."

"I've heard profanity in elementary school and that's not a book's fault. If your children are raised right, this book is not going to affect your children. But this is the real world. This is the 1990s. We read books to gain knowledge and I commend students and teachers for doing that. Just keep it going."

Sunday school teacher Penny Owens quoted Bible verses, saying she wanted the committee to know what God says about such books.

"But if anyone causes one of these little ones who believe in me to sin, it would be better for him to have a large millstone hung around his neck and to be drown [sic] in the depths of the sea," said Ms. Owens, quoting Matthew 18:6.

Greg Standridge, a pastor at a local church, said he admires the author for what she has been able to accomplish and he enjoyed reading part of the book, but other passages "made my stomach roll over several times."

Standridge said if the sexual passages in the book were on television, he would turn it off because he doesn't want "this kind of thing to get into their minds. This can get into their minds. Some can handle it and some cannot . . . some children will deeply meditate on this."

Ms. McCleskey questioned the point of reading the book and the motives of teachers who use it.

"You can't treat all children like they are abused children," she said. "You don't throw all these children into group therapy."

Parent Dallas Letson said he read the book so he could address the committee, but he didn't have to read the whole book "to find the filth

in it." He said other optional books were thicker so students opted for the thinner book by Angelou.

Diane Stanridge said her daughter said, " 'This book is nasty.' "

Senior Justin Mattli, editor of the school's literary magazine "Eagle Feathers," urged parents "to keep an open mind."

"Times are changing," said Mattli. "It might not be this way in Lawrence County, but out in other places there is rape—and you can't sugar-coat rape."

If Thomas isn't satisfied with the school committee's decision, he can appeal it to the county media committee, then the school board. The committee is composed of parents, teachers, a librarian, the principal and a student.

LESLEY FARREY PACEY, "BOOK BAN TURNED DOWN: TEACHERS WHO SUPPORTED BOOK SAY THEY ARE BEING HARASSED" (*Decatur Daily*, March 19, 1996, A1+)

CADDO—A school media committee has sent a parent a letter telling him the committee won't ban poet Maya Angelou's critically acclaimed auto-biography, "I Know Why The Caged Bird Sings," from required reading at East Lawrence High School.

If parent George F. Thomas wants to continue his effort, he will have until March 29 to appeal to the county media committee. The appeal from there is the school board. His wife said he is out of town and una-vailable for comment.

The 12-member media committee decided Angelou's book, which was only required for senior advanced placement (college level) students, should be required reading for all high school honors, advanced place-ment and pre-advanced placement English classes.

The committee also decided students in all other English classes can continue using the book as supplemental reading material. Those stu-dents will be given at least one optional reading assignment.

The book was optional reading for ninth-graders who could choose between it and the Charles Dickens classic, "Great Expectations," said media committee chairwoman Anita Bowling. People who want the book banned said that is untrue and the school only made it optional for ninth-graders after Thomas complained. . . .

The committee deliberated for an hour and 15 minutes March 12 after an emotional hearing at East Lawrence High School, where nine of 13 speakers backed Thomas' appeal. A deputy stood outside the door and patrolled the front parking area.

But since the meeting, teachers who are against the ban say they have been harassed.

An East Lawrence High School biology teacher who backed the book at the hearing, said a man accosted her in the rear parking lot after the meeting.

An English teacher who uses the book said she noticed a car following her home so she detoured to a grocery store.

Ms. Bowling said that she and the two teachers have received late-night, hang-up telephone calls as have two students who spoke against banning the book.

She is chairwoman of the school's English department and president of the Lawrence County Language Arts Teachers Association.

"We are just trying to do our jobs," said Ms. Bowling. "We don't plan to put up with this harassment."

She said the school media committee considered parents' concerns about sexual passages and profane language, but was influenced more by a college board recommendation to use the author and poet's book in all high school advanced placement classes.

"The committee wants to recognize the parental prerogative," she said. "But with the children on the honors and the AP track, it's difficult to meet our instructional objectives if we can't use the [AP] suggested works."

"It's our job to make sure students have a quality educational experience," she said. . . .

Thomas filed an appeal on the book in December along with a 21-page petition bearing about 500 signatures after Superintendent Patrick Graham, acting in violation of school board policy, attempted to ban the book himself.

Thomas said the day after the East Lawrence hearing that he hoped the school committee based its decision on "what the community wants." He said the petition proves many concerned parents don't believe the book is appropriate for required reading.

But Ms. Bowling said she found "numerous discrepancies" in the petition, including names from outside the East Lawrence school district, names listed more than once, different signatures in the same handwriting and a dead person's name.

"This document is flawed beyond belief," Ms. Bowling said. "But even if it wasn't flawed, no special importance would be given to it."

Thomas said after the hearing that he didn't like how Ms. Bowling and the media committee treated him by limiting time for speakers to five minutes. Thirteen people spoke at the hearing. Thomas was also unhappy that the four people who spoke against the ban, spoke last.

The day after the hearing biology teacher Michelle Cleveland filed a complaint with the Lawrence County Sheriff's Department. She said a man wearing a houndstooth check hat, a trench coat and dark glasses and [*sic*] grabbed her arm from behind as she was getting a calculator from her car in the rear parking area after the meeting.

"He said, 'I have to talk to you.' I told him, 'Not until you let go of my arm.' "

When the man released her she said she walked back into the building as he shouted insults, used racial slurs and called her "immoral."

"He said he could not understand how someone could teach students and not be for banning the book," she said. . . .

Ms. Cleveland said she received hang-up telephone calls until 4:30 a.m. "I'm definitely watching my moves these days."

English teacher Ernestine Robinson is at the center of the controversy because she fought attempts to ban the book from her optional reading list for ninth-graders when Thomas went to the superintendent.

"I'm almost very, very certain I was followed" from the school Tuesday night for more than 10 miles. "Maybe they were trying to scare me, but I'm a hard nut to crack."

She drove to a grocery store parking lot and went inside.

Ms. Robinson said that she and two other teachers on the committee were the only blacks at the hearing attended by about 40 people[.] She said some parents fighting the book have a "white agenda."

The committee voted by secret ballot with nine members voting for the change, two members voting to make no changes and one unable to decide, Ms. Bowling said. The committee is made up of four teachers, a librarian, a student and parents equal to the number of school employees.

Ms. Robinson is on the committee, but she didn't vote because teachers would have outnumbered parents, Ms. Bowling said.

LESLEY FARREY PACEY, "PARENT STILL WANTS BOOK BANNED"
(*Decatur Daily*, April 5, 1996)

MOULTON—The "Caged Bird" isn't free yet.

After a school media committee turned down his attempt to ban Maya Angelou's autobiography, "I Know Why the Caged Bird Sings," parent George F. Thomas is taking his appeal to the next level.

Thomas is asking the Lawrence County School System Media Committee to hear his appeal to remove Angelou's critically acclaimed book from required reading.

Teresa Culbert, library media coordinator, said Thomas filed to continue his appeal in a letter sent days after the East Lawrence High School media committee returned its decision. Thomas could not be reached for comment. . . .

Ms. Culbert said this is the first time the school system media committee has received an appeal since the book banning policy, setting up a procedure for banning books, was adopted in spring 1988.

The system media committee is made up of Ms. Culbert, the school system secondary supervisor, a secondary principal (not from East Lawrence), one high school librarian, a high school teacher, a student and a member from each high school community.

LESLEY FARREY PACEY, "WITH 'AMENS,' BAN URGED ON BOOK: ONLY TWO SPEAK IN FAVOR OF 'BIRD' AT SECOND HEARING"
(Decatur Daily, June 18, 1996, A1+)

MOULTON—Once again, a hearing on a parent's attempt to remove Maya Angelou's autobiography from required reading played out like a church revival.

At the second hearing this year on George F. Thomas' appeal of "I Know Why the Caged Bird Sings," preachers and lay people quoted scripture, parents warned of the evils of pornography they say is contained in the book and audience members interjected amens during speeches they liked.

But at this hearing, the crowd—stung by not getting what they wanted from the East Lawrence school media committee at a March hearing—was louder and larger than before.

About 75 people, about twice the number at the March hearing, filled the auditorium of the Lawrence County Board of Education and spilled into the halls Monday. Most clearly supported Thomas, rising for a standing ovation after his speech and clapping loudly after speakers with similar views spoke.

Those who favored the book were fewer and quieter. Only two of 15 speakers spoke in favor of the book and both were East Lawrence High School teachers.

Thomas should know this week if power in numbers pays. The system media committee deliberated in private for 1 ½ hours after the hearing that lasted the same length of time before reaching a decision that was not made public. They were to mail their decision today by certified mail to Thomas. If he isn't satisfied with that decision, he can appeal to the school board. . . .

At Monday night's hearing, Thomas said he wants the book removed from required reading because some passages about growing up as a black female in rural Arkansas in the 1930s, aren't appropriate reading for students.

Thomas, whose daughter was in an honors ninth-grade class last school year at East Lawrence, said certain passages are too sexually explicit, including one in which Ms. Angelou is raped as a child by her mother's boyfriend.

"This is where I was first shocked by the explicit and graphic manner in which the molestation and rape was described and I . . ." Thomas said, pausing for a breath, hands shaking and voice cracking as he apologized for what he was about to describe.

After he read the passage he said:

"I ask you if these few paragraphs I have described were a scene in a movie, what would the rating be? Would it be suitable for kids? This book is riddled with excerpts that pertain to perverted sexual conduct."

Thomas also said he was opposed to a scene in which a young Ms. Angelou watches as her "11-year-old brother has sex with a 15-year-old girl" and one chapter where Ms. Angelou wonders if she is a lesbian before having sex with a man and getting pregnant.

"I want you to understand that teaching this type of material undermines my parental authority," he said. "By teaching that homosexuality is OK, homosexuals are the way they are because of a physical condition that they have no control over—this is wrong and you can't teach that."

As other speakers alluded to the same scenes, they called them "pornographic" and "trash" and questioned the power they have over young minds.

Dallas Letson, a father and grandfather, said, "things like this book will put ideas" into young boys and girls' heads.

Anthony Simmons, an East Lawrence High School graduate, said, "By using this material to help cope with students and what they've been exposed to, could it not as well cause setbacks and flashbacks to victims as well as influence others who are sexually aggressive? The children's lives are so valuable we should not play with them. Let's teach them."

Gordon Ray, a local church elder, urged teachers to think about the harm the book may cause.

"The statement has been made that maybe you can help one child overcome an offensive home life or what have you, but what about the 99 other children that you influence to do something wrong? What about those that come from the good homes and you influence them to experiment with pornography or sex or lesbianism or some other sin?"

Ray commended Superintendent Patrick Graham for trying to remove the book after parents complained and urged the committee to do the same. Thomas filed an appeal on the book in December after Graham, acting in violation of school board policy, attempted to ban the book himself.

"I plead with you good and honest teachers to hold fast to the one book that will save souls and displace any and all books that teach or show ungodly acts. I feel that Mr. Graham may not have followed proper procedure, but why hold onto trash to prove a point?"

Peggy McCleskey, a parent and church youth director, questioned the judgment of teachers who use the book.

"I find it inexcusable that any adult would force pornography on a child—yet that is exactly what is happening every time a child is required to read the book in question tonight. This book is filled with profanity and obscenity and any adult requiring this [to be] read by a child lacks good sound judgment."

But Anita Bowling, chairwoman of the East Lawrence school media committee, said the system media committee should think about students and not "special interest groups" when they vote on Thomas' appeal. She said it would be unfair to remove the book which is recommended by the state for nine-12 honors students.

Science teacher Michelle Cleveland said the book isn't pornographic because it does not fit the definition of pornography: material "intended to arouse sexual excitement" and considered to have "little or no artistic merit."

"Needless to say, I do not believe the violation of Maya is intended to sexually arouse the reader. Hence it is not pornography in any way, shape or form. To say so is a slander against the book and against the author."

She said the book is intended rather to inspire. "[This] is an autobiography describing the adversities in life she had to overcome to become one of the most renowned black authors of our time. It is a story that can give the reader inspiration—inspiration through knowing that whatever life gives a person good or bad, that person can accomplish whatever he or she set out to do."

English teacher Ernestine Robinson, who is at the center of the controversy because she fought attempts to remove the book from her optional reading list for ninth graders when Thomas went to the superintendent, did not attend because she was sick.

LESLEY FARREY PACEY, "ANGELOU STORY OPTIONS GIVEN"
(*Decatur Daily*, June 22, 1996, A1+)

MOULTON—Six months after filing his first appeal, an East Lawrence parent's attempt to remove Maya Angelou's autobiography from required reading is successful.

A 12-member Lawrence County school system media committee has decided that "I Know Why the Caged Bird Sings" may be assigned by any teacher in grades nine through 12. But if the teacher assigns the book, another of comparable literary value must be available to students whose parents object to the book.

Teresa Culbert, county media committee chairwoman, said she hopes the decision which affects all seven high schools in the county makes parents and teachers happy.

"We came up with what we thought was the best for all," she said.

Parent George F. Thomas could not be reached for comment. Ms. Culbert said Thomas received the system committee's decision by certified mail this week. If he isn't satisfied with the decision, he can make a final appeal to the school board.

"LAWRENCE COUNTY PARENT RENEWS EFFORT TO BAN BOOK"
(Decatur Daily, July 5, 1996)

MOULTON—A parent plans to renew his efforts to get poet Maya Angelou's autobiography banned from a school's optional reading list to the Lawrence County school board.

George Thomas, whose child attends East Lawrence High School, said he isn't satisfied with the decision by the county school system's media committee to allow "I Know Why the Caged Bird Sings" to remain on the school reading list. He plans to appeal to the county school board. . . .

Some parents in the past have objected to the book. They also objected when the word "banned" was used, saying they only wanted to keep students from being required to read the book. . . .

The tentative date to hear the appeal is Aug. 5, during the board's meeting, Graham said. Media committee chairwoman Teresa Culbert said she was surprised Thomas is appealing the decision.

Lawrence education board member Charles Satchel said Thomas can take the matter to the county's circuit court if he's not satisfied with the board's decision.

CLYDE L. STANCIL, "GRAHAM WANTS POWER TO REMOVE QUESTIONABLE BOOKS UNTIL FINAL APPEAL"
(Decatur Daily, September 4, 1996, A1+)

MOULTON—The Lawrence County superintendent wants himself and principals to have the authority to remove any questionable reading material from their schools until all review appeals have been finalized.

Superintendent Patrick Graham said the present procedure to remove books takes took [*sic*] long. The procedure, in some cases, can include an appeal to two media committees and the school board.

"The way the policy is written at this point is that when any book is being appealed by the parent, it takes about a year to [settle the matter]," said Graham. "It would remain on the required list and the students will be required to read it."

Graham's request to the school board is in response to the length of time it's taking to finalize a decision on Maya Angelou's "I Know Why the Caged Bird Sings."

A parent of an East Lawrence High School student and his supporters objected to some of the language in the book. After failing to win satisfaction from either the school's Media Committee or the system's Media Committee, the parent will present his request to the school board. No date has been set for the meeting.

Graham said board members have the authority to readjust the policy because they implemented the procedures.

Board member Charles Satchel said he's seen the proposed revision of the policy but said he doesn't agree with the changes.

"We have a mechanism in place for checks and balances," said Satchel. "So one person, be it the superintendent or the principal, should not have that kind of authority. We should leave the mechanism there that's already in place, and let them decide. Of course all of these books are on the approved list of state reading. If a book is on the list, then I don't have a problem with it."

But Graham disagrees and said the yearlong appeal process is detrimental to the morale of parents, and the morals of children.

"Some books may go against what the Bible teaches as far as moral values," said Graham. "In fact, in the Bible, it teaches that you shouldn't even talk about some of the things that are done is [*sic*] secret. Some parents are teaching their children that way. And it wouldn't be right for their children to read those things."

Graham said the public school system has been continually losing support from parents and the schools need to find ways to increase that support. He said a vote to allow "Caged Bird" to remain on the reading list "won't help a bit."

"It will really hurt us more as far as our support from parents," Graham said. "In fact, the new foundation's program is trying to emphasize getting parents involved, and I think that when you start alienating parents, we're going in reverse. Especially when they are right, and I think they are right on this case."

Should the board grant approval, "Caged Bird" will not be affected by the decision.

CLYDE L. STANCIL, "BOOK CHANGE MAY BRING LAWSUIT"
(*Decatur Daily*, September 24, 1996)

MOULTON—The local director of the Alabama Educational Association threatened to sue the Lawrence County school board for any written changes in policy it approves without consulting him.

AEA's UniServe District 4 director Walt Maddox said he has sent two letters to Superintendent Patrick Graham asking for notification of pending changes in the textbook selection policy.

Maddox, speaking at Monday night's Lawrence County Board of Education meeting, referred to a hearing that was held after the meeting on whether or not the board would remove Maya Angelou's controversial book "I Know Why the Caged Bird Sings" from the county's required reading list.

"When a sensitive issue of this sort arises, sometimes the due process of formulating board policy can be overlooked," said Maddox. He quoted the Code of Alabama as saying that " 'before adopting the written policies, the board shall directly or indirectly, through the chief executive officer, consult with the applicable local employees' professional organization.' "

AEA is a teachers' organization. Maddox said he expects to receive written notice before the board makes any changes and to be given an opportunity to respond. He said any decision on policy change of which he is not a part is void.

"Lastly, let me encourage you to work diligently with the Language Arts Association in Lawrence County and exploit their talent and expertise," said Maddox. ". . . I have received numerous calls from my members concerning the action this board is about to take."

He was referring to complaints from his members who support the book, who disputed claims that the book has no redeemable value.

"I hope that by bringing this matter to your attention, we can work together for an equitable solution," he said.

Graham, interviewed after the meeting, did not directly answer Maddox's complaint. He said he thought the board ought to respond to parents' desires.

"A good decision like this [parental objection to the book], I'll honor that," said Graham. "A bad decision, we'll talk about that."

"I'm saying any book that has the language that this book has in it, I don't care who wrote it or where they're from, our kids don't need to be reading it," said Graham. "I don't think Jesus would like it."

CLYDE L. STANCIL, "LAWRENCE BOARD NEARS LAST CHAPTER
OF 'CAGED' DEBATE"
(*Decatur Daily*, September 24, 1996)

MOULTON—The final chapter in the attempt to remove a controversial book from the county schools' required reading list will be closed Oct. 7 when the Lawrence school board renders its decision.

"I will be satisfied with the board's decision," said George Thomas. "I feel the board will uphold our view on this 100 percent because our view lines up exactly with the appeals procedure." . . .

The board must decide whether to remove the book completely from county schools or give objecting students and parents another option.

More than 60 people and media personnel attended the book hearing at the Lawrence County Board of Education office building Monday night, expecting the board to make a decision. But before announcing the 13 people who would voice their opposition or support for the book, board Chairman Wendell Logan said the decision would not be rendered until the board's next meeting.

Supporters of removal of the book—many of whom questioned teacher Ernestine Robinson's character for introducing the book to students—came to the hearing with a sense of renewed vigor.

Marsha Garrie of Caddo produced a list of books allegedly on the state and county reading lists. She said Ms. Angelou's book does not appear on them.

Thomas had a similar list he said was obtained from Lawrence schools' secondary education supervisor, Jim Addison.

"I haven't checked it out, so I couldn't verify it either way," said Superintendent Patrick Graham on whether the book is on either list. He said he didn't know if any other school in the county was using the book.

Board member Wade Harrison said, "I know it was on the list that I was sent."

Thomas also disputed a claim that copies of the book were purchased with county money. He said his daughter was given a deadline to have the money in for purchase of the book.

Although the author, Ms. Angelou, and the teacher, Mrs. Robinson, are both black, Graham said the debate is not racial. He said black parents from Courtland viewed the book and also thought it unsuitable for children.

Graham has been steadfast in his opinion that the book goes against biblical teachings and should not be read by students. He went to East Lawrence on Nov. 20 last year and demanded the book's removal.

Mrs. Robinson reminded the almost all-white audience, who said they were Christians, that she has gone to jail to have books containing blacks put in the schools.

"Please do not misconstrue this statement," said Mrs. Robinson, a former civil rights activist. "But if there is a place for me beside some of you in heaven, I choose hell."

Thomas officially voiced his opposition to the book Dec. 7 when his daughter brought some of its sexually explicit content to his attention. He said he tried to contact Mrs. Robinson to no avail.

Since that time, Thomas has been through two hearings where his requests to have the book removed entirely from the county's reading list have failed. . . .

Thomas insists that he is not trying to have the book "banned" from county schools.

"The appeals procedure provides us with the right to appeal this book, and we're not trying to do anything that's not provided for in the appeals procedure," said Thomas. "The appeals procedure gives us the right to appeal this or any book we feel is not appropriate for our children."

CLYDE L. STANCIL, "LAWRENCE SCHOOLS OK 'BIRD' FOR BOOK LIST"
(*Decatur Daily*, October 8, 1996, A1+)

MOULTON—Disappointed supporters of an effort to remove a controversial book from a required reading list in Lawrence County filed out of a Monday meeting after the school board voted 3–2 against removal.

About 60 people—for and against—waited for the county Board of Education to return from an unrelated closed hearing to announce a decision on Maya Angelou's "I Know Why the Caged Bird Sings."

The vote was taken without any discussion among board members, in contrast to the fanfare that had accompanied three previous hearings to appeal the use of the book, which opponents deemed sexually explicit and unsuitable for children.

"I think the book should have been removed," said East Lawrence High School parent Anita Flannagin. "I don't think it's suited for any high school person to read. I think it goes against my values and the morals that I'm trying to teach my children, and I'm very disappointed in the three (board members) that voted to leave it in there. My daughter is not going to read the book . . . she's made that very clear."

Board members Charles Satchel, Wade Harrison and Hollis Thompson voted against the motion to remove the book. The book is assigned to students in grades 9–12 who are in advanced-placement English. Chairman Wendell Logan and James Cheatham voted for the motion.

"I read the book, and I just don't think it should be required reading for any student," said Cheatham. "They can go to the library to check it out if they want to read it."

The board's decision to keep the book on the county's list—opponents had produced state and county lists that didn't show the book—means the countywide media committee's decision stands. The committee allowed anyone who objects to the book an option to be assigned another book.

"The only thing [wrong] with an option like it's left now is that a teacher can (assign) a book with twice as many pages," said Cheatham. "When you give that as an option, students are going to take the smaller book."

George Thomas, the parent who filed the original appeal, was absent from the audience. At an Oct. 7 hearing before the board, Thomas said he would abide by the board's decision, because he felt sure "the board will uphold our views 100 percent."

Instead, the board sided with the decision first upheld by an East Lawrence media committee. Thomas filed an appeal Dec. 7 when his daughter brought some of the book's sexually explicit material to his attention.

Before filing his appeal, Thomas said he tried in vain to contact his daughter's English teacher, Ernestine Robinson, and then contacted Superintendent Patrick Graham.

Graham went to East Lawrence on Nov. 20 last year and demanded that the book be removed because, in his opinion, it was against biblical teachings.

"I wish [the board] had gone with my recommendations," said Graham. "I was down on my knees when I asked the Lord what I should recommend, and that's what I did."

But not everyone thought the book was full of evil content.

"I didn't see anything that was so hideous that it deserved to be removed from the reading list," said the Rev. Lee Langham, president of the Lawrence County National Association for the Advancement of Colored People. "They have an option. If they want to read it, they can go to their parents and ask for permission to read the book. And if the parents have an objection to them reading the book, they don't read it."

The board's policy does not require parent approval before the book is assigned, however.

"In talking to my daughter, she doesn't feel that the book is [unsuitable]," said Hilman Locklayer, an East Lawrence parent. "I've started reading it—I'm about half way through—and really haven't run up on anything in there that would justify [keeping the book off the list]."

STUDY QUESTIONS

1. Define censorship.

2. According to the first document in this chapter from *Attacks on the Freedom to Learn: 1996 Report*, what are some of the general trends in censorship attacks? Discuss, for example, the frequency of attacks, the success rates of would-be censors, the targets of their attacks, the leaders of the attacks, and the basis for their objections.

3. What are the most common reasons given for challenging Angelou's autobiography?

4. From your reading of the various documents in this chapter, what has been the overall success rate of censorship attacks on *I Know Why the Caged Bird Sings*?

5. In the East Lawrence High School controversy, what are the specific objections of those who oppose *I Know Why the Caged Bird Sings*? What are the specific arguments of those who support the work?

TOPICS FOR WRITTEN OR ORAL EXPLORATION

1. According to Beach and Marshall, what assumptions do would-be censors make about literary texts? Do you agree or disagree with their assumptions? Why or why not?

2. In your opinion, why have African American women writers been the subject of an increasing number of censorship attempts?

3. In your analysis of one or two of the cases presented in this study, what factors contributed to the success or failure of the censorship attempt?

4. From the various cases and their resolutions, what do you think are the most effective policies for dealing with censorship? Justify your response.

5. Research your school's own policies and procedures for dealing with censorship attacks. In light of the experiences of other schools discussed in this chapter, are your school's policies and procedures adequate? If not, what changes would you suggest?

6. Stage a debate between a would-be censor of *I Know Why the Caged Bird Sings* and an opponent of censorship of the work.

7. Imagine that you are a student at East Lawrence High School at the time of the banning attempt. Write a letter to the editor in which you respond to the controversy.

8. Write a paper in which you analyze the specific philosophies motivating the leaders on both sides of the East Lawrence controversy over *I Know Why the Caged Bird Sings*. What are their views on education, parental authority, adolescent behavior, etc.?

WORKS CITED

Beach, Richard W., and James D. Marshall. *Teaching Literature in the Secondary School*. San Diego: Harcourt Brace Jovanovich, 1991.

Foerstel, Herbert N. *Banned in the U.S.A.: A Reference Guide to Book Censorship in Schools and Public Libraries*. Westport, Conn.: Greenwood Press, 1994.

"Maya Angelou's 'Most Challenged' Book." *American Libraries* 27, 3 (March 1996): 5.

SUGGESTED READINGS

See the full text of works excerpted in this chapter and other publications of People for the American Way and the American Library Association's Office for Intellectual Freedom.

Goodale, Gloria. "Censorship vs. Parental Discretion: Who Decides Which Books a Child May Read?" *Christian Science Monitor*, December 6, 1996, 11.

Johnson, Claudia Durst. *Understanding "To Kill a Mockingbird."* Westport, Conn.: Greenwood Press, 1994. (See, in particular, the questions at the end of Chapter 6, "The Issue of Censorship.")

Parker, Barbara, and Stefanie Weiss. *Protecting the Freedom to Learn: A Citizen's Guide*. Washington, D.C.: People for the American Way, 1983.

For more information on the antihumanist views of the religious right, see:

LaHaye, Tim. *The Battle for the Mind*. Old Tappan, N.J.: Fleming H. Revell, 1980.

Bibliographic Essay

This essay considers some of the important events in Angelou's life beginning with the years following the birth of her son (the point where *I Know Why the Caged Bird Sings* concludes) and ending with her most recent activities and honors. Sources for these remarks include Angelou's own autobiographical accounts, a biography of Angelou, interviews, newspaper articles, an essay, timelines, publicity materials, and the Internet.

Angelou's second autobiography, *Gather Together in My Name*, was published in 1974. The book begins with a discussion of the hope African Americans had for better race relations at the end of World War II and the subsequent disappointment of those hopes. In *Order out of Chaos: The Autobiographical Works of Maya Angelou*, Dolly McPherson notes that the character of this political moment is consistent with Angelou's own story: "The fragmented texture of the larger American society at the end of World War II serves as an appropriate backdrop for the reader's introduction to the alienated and fragmented nature of Angelou's life" (622–63). Angelou details a series of odd jobs she takes to support herself and her infant son: restaurant jobs, including Creole cook, waitress, bus girl, fry cook, and manager; and even odder jobs, including madam, dancer, prostitute, and chauffeurette. During this period she returns to Stamps for a brief, ill-fated visit (her hasty departure is described in Chapter 2 of this study); she is turned down for the army on the grounds that she attended a school on the House Un-American Activities Committee list; and she continues to study dance. When she considers trying hard drugs, a friend generously exposes Angelou to the horrors of drug addiction by bringing her to a hit joint for heroin addicts. His actions have the desired outcome, as Angelou ends the book with a fervent promise never again to lose her newfound innocence.

Singin' and Swingin' and Gettin' Merry Like Christmas (1976), the next book in her five-volume autobiographical series, opens in 1949 with Maya landing a job as sales clerk in a record store. Here she meets Tosh Angelos, a white sailor, whom she marries "because he asked" (25). When her suffocating marriage ends after two years, she finds work, first as a dancer in a strip joint, and then in a cabaret singing calypso (it is in this job that her name is changed from Angelos to Angelou, "an exotic-sounding corruption of her married name" [Shapiro, 89]). Her big break comes in 1954 when she is cast in the role of Ruby, a dancer-singer part in a touring company production of *Porgy and Bess*. The troupe's travels to eastern and western Europe and North Africa expose Angelou to a wide variety of languages and cultures. The title of the autobiography is suggestive of the camaraderie and rich social life she enjoys with the troupe's cast and many locals. According to McPherson, these experiences "expand and complicate [Angelou's] understanding of the complexities of race relations" (85). After months on tour Angelou learns that her son is ill. She returns to San Francisco, guilt-ridden at having left Guy for so long. The volume closes in 1955 with mother and son together in Hawaii, where Angelou has again found work as an entertainer, and with Angelou's celebration of her "wonderful, dependently independent son" (242). McPherson writes: "While *Singin' and Swingin'* is certainly a praisesong to *Porgy and Bess*, it is also a love song to Angelou's son, who grows up over the course of its pages" (89).

Angelou begins the fourth volume of her autobiography, *The Heart of a Woman*, published in 1981, with a discussion of the contradictions of black-white relations in 1957 and her brief membership in the "beatnik brigade" (3). She meets the legendary Billie Holiday. In 1959 she moves to New York to become part of the Harlem Writers Guild, where her early writing receives the valuable and sometimes harsh critiques of the other members of the guild. She appears at the famous Apollo Theatre, "long the most prestigious venue for black entertainers," according to Miles Shapiro (93). With Godfrey Cambridge, Angelou produces the "Cabaret for Freedom" in 1960 to benefit Martin Luther King and the Southern Christian Leadership Conference (SCLC). She publishes her first short story in a Cuban publication. She becomes the Northern Coordinator for the SCLC and meets Martin Luther King, Malcolm X, and South African freedom fighter Vusumzi (Vus) Make. Although they never formally wed, Angelou and Make soon consider themselves to be husband and wife. In

1960 she stars with James Earl Jones, Lou Gossett Jr., Cicely Tyson, and other important African American actors in Jean Genet's *The Blacks*, with Angelou in the role of the White Queen. She composes some of the music for the play. During this period, Angelou is a founding member of The Cultural Association for Women of African Heritage, which organizes a protest at the United Nations on the occasion of the death of the president of the Congo, Patrice Lumumba. The *New York Times* front page description of the event includes the following headline: "Riot in Gallery Halts U.N. Debate: American Negroes Ejected after Invading Session" (February 16, 1961). Angelou, Guy, and Vus move to Egypt after being evicted from their New York apartment when Vus fails to pay the rent. To prevent a second eviction in Cairo, Angelou finds a job as associate editor of a magazine, the *Arab Observer*, and later writes reviews for Radio Egypt. When her marriage ends due to Make's infidelity and his narrow views regarding the role of the wife of an African, Angelou moves to Ghana so that Guy can attend the University of Ghana. After Guy is seriously injured in an automobile accident, she finds employment at the university as an administrative assistant at the School of Music and Drama in order to be able to care for Guy during his convalescence. The book ends with her son once again establishing his independence as he moves into his new dormitory room, and with Angelou relishing the fact that she will now "be able to eat the whole breast of a roast chicken by [her]self" (272).

The most recent of Angelou's autobiographical works, *All God's Children Need Traveling Shoes* (1986), opens with a return to the painful, lonely days and weeks following Guy's accident. Although Angelou had intended to take a job in Liberia with the Department of Information, Guy's accident keeps her in Ghana. According to Dolly McPherson, Angelou has other reasons for staying in Ghana: "the need to leave Egypt, following her broken marriage to Vusumzi Make, and her decision to bring up her son in a country of Blacks governed by Blacks" (105). Angelou soon falls in love with Ghana and its people and develops a close relationship with other black Americans living there. During this period, Angelou grows disaffected with Martin Luther King's philosophy ("We were brave revolutionaries, not pussyfooting nonviolent cowards" [121]); nevertheless, in 1963 she and her radical friends march on the American Embassy in Ghana in sympathy with a march led by King on Washington, D.C. In Ghana, Angelou again meets Malcolm X after his 1964 trip to the Islamic holy city of Mecca. She is invited to Berlin and Venice to reprise her role in *The Blacks*. She returns to Egypt and is asked to sing for Liberia's president. When Malcolm X needs a coordinator for the Organization of Afro-American Unity and Guy declares that she has "finished mothering a child" (185), Angelou decides to return to the United States. At the airport in Accra she reflects that while she is leaving Africa, she is

not sad, "for now I knew my people had never completely left Africa. . . .
As we carried it to Philadelphia, Boston and Birmingham we had changed
its color, modified its rhythms, yet it was Africa which rode in the bulges
of our high calves, shook in our protruding behinds and crackled in our
wide open laughter. I could nearly hear the old ones chuckling" (208).

Thus ends Angelou's own autobiographical accounts. In a 1987 interview Angelou declared that she plans to write one more volume, "bringing us up to the publication of 'Caged Bird' then go no further. 'After
that it would just be writing about writing which is something I don't
want to do' " (Webster). While we await the final volume of her autobiography, we are forced to turn to other sources for the events that follow
Angelou's 1965 departure from Africa.

Chronology of Maya Angelou's Career

1966   Angelou produces her play *The Least of These*.
        Appears in *Medea*.

1967   Writes her play *Gettin' Up Stayed On My Mind*.

1968   Writes, produces, and narrates a ten-part television series, *Black! Blues! Black!*, for National Educational Television.

1970   Publishes *I Know Why the Caged Bird Sings*, which is nominated for a National Book Award.
        Appointed Writer-in-Residence, University of Kansas in Lawrence.

1971   Publishes her first collection of poetry, *Just Give Me a Cool Drink of Water 'Fore I Diiie*. The collection is nominated for a Pulitzer Prize in 1972.

1972   Writes the screenplay and music for the film *Georgia, Georgia*.

1973   Plays the role of Mrs. Keckley in *Look Away* on Broadway. She receives a Tony Award nomination for her performance.
        Marries Paul Du Feu. They are divorced in 1981.

1974   Publishes *Gather Together in My Name*.
        Adapts Sophocles' *Ajax*, which premiers in Los Angeles.
        Writes the screenplay for and directs *All Day Long*.
        Appointed Distinguished Visiting Professor at Wichita State University, California State University, Sacramento, and Wake Forest University.

1975   Publishes her next poetry collection, *Oh Pray My Wings Are Gonna Fit Me Well*.
        Appointed by President Gerald Ford to the American Revolution Bicentennial Council.
        Writes six half-hour programs, "Assignment America," which premiers in January.

1976   Publishes *Singin' and Swingin' and Gettin' Merry Like Christmas*.
        Writes and directs a musical play, *And Still I Rise*.
        Writes and hosts two programs for the United States Information Agency, "The Legacy" and "The Inheritors."
        Receives Woman of the Year Award in Communications from the *Ladies' Home Journal*.

1977   Has a supporting role as Kunta Kinte's grandmother, Nyo Boto, in Alex Haley's *Roots*. Receives an Emmy Award nomination for Best Supporting Actress for her performance.
        Wins the Golden Eagle Award for "Afro-American in the Arts," a documentary broadcast on PBS.

1978   Publishes her third collection of poetry, *And Still I Rise*.
        Serves on Jimmy Carter's Presidential Commission for International Women's Year.

1979   Co-authors the adaptation of *I Know Why the Caged Bird Sings*, broadcast on CBS.

1981   Publishes *The Heart of a Woman*.
        Accepts a lifetime appointment as Reynolds Professor of American Studies at Wake Forest University.

1982   Writes and produces the film *Sister, Sister*, shown on NBC.

1983   Publishes her fourth collection of poems, *Shaker, Why Don't You Sing?*
        Premiere of her play *On a Southern Journey*.

1986   Publishes *All God's Children Need Traveling Shoes*.

1987   Publishes her collection of poems *Now Sheba Sings the Song*, illustrated by Tom Feelings.

1988   Directs Errol John's play *Moon on a Rainbow Shawl*.

1990   Publishes her collection of poems *I Shall Not Be Moved*.

1993   Recites her poem "On the Pulse of Morning" at President Bill Clinton's inauguration, for which she receives a Grammy Award (Best Spoken Word Album) in 1994.
        Publishes her personal essay *Wouldn't Take Nothing for My Journey Now*.

Publishes her first children's book, *Life Doesn't Frighten Me* (a poem).

Appears in the television movie *There Are No Children Here*.

1994   Publishes her next children's book, *My Painted House, My Friendly Chicken and Me*.

1995   Publishes *Phenomenal Woman: Four Poems for Women*.

Recites "A Brave and Startling Truth" at the celebration of the fiftieth anniversary of the United Nations.

Delivers the poem "From a Black Woman to a Black Man" at the Million Man March in Washington, D.C.

Appears in an episode of the television series *Touched by an Angel*.

Appears in the movie *How to Make an American Quilt*.

1996   Publishes her third children's book, *Kofi and His Magic*.

Re-releases "Miss Calypso" (first recorded in 1957).

Appointed an ambassador of UNICEF International.

1997   Writes "Extravagant Spirits" (poetry) for *Life* magazine's Collector's Edition.

Publishes a collection of personal essays, *Even the Stars Look Lonesome*.

WORKS CONSULTED

Angelou, Maya. *All God's Children Need Traveling Shoes*. New York: Random House, 1986.

———. *Gather Together in My Name*. New York: Random House, 1974.

———. *The Heart of a Woman*. New York: Random House, 1981.

———. *Singin' and Swingin' and Gettin' Merry Like Christmas*. 1976. Toronto: Bantam Books, 1977.

Elliot, Jeffrey M., ed. *Conversations with Maya Angelou*. Jackson: University Press of Mississippi, 1989.

Lordly & Dame, Inc. Publicity materials for Maya Angelou. 51 Church Street, Boston, MA 02116–5493.

McMahon, Thomas, ed. *Authors and Artists for Young Adults*. Detroit: Gale, 1997.

McPherson, Dolly A. *Order Out of Chaos: The Autobiographical Works of Maya Angelou*. New York: Peter Lang, 1990.

"Riot in Gallery Halts U.N. Debate: American Negroes Ejected after Invading Session—Midtown March Balked." *New York Times*, February 16, 1961, A1+.

Shapiro, Miles. *Maya Angelou*. New York: Chelsea House, 1994.

Webster, Valerie. "A Journey Through Life." *Yorkshire Post*, July 27, 1987.

Index

About the Author

JOANNE MEGNA-WALLACE is Professor of Humanities at Bradford College in Bradford, Massachusetts, where she teaches French and women's literature. She is the author of articles on Maya Angelou, Jean-Paul Sartre, and Simone de Beauvoir. Her current interests include francophone and ethnic literatures, especially African American women's literature.